Phil Reimer's B.C. Weather Book

Phil Reimer's B.C. Weather Book

Phil Reimer
with
Sean Rossiter

Phil Reimer Communications
Vancouver

Phil Reimer Communications
P.O. Box 2141
Vancouver, B.C.
V6B 3T8

Canadian Cataloguing in Publication Data

Reimer, Phil, 1941-
Phil Reimer's B.C. weather book

Includes bibliographical references and index.
ISBN 0-9695380-0-6

1. British Columbia–Climate–Popular works.
2. Lower Mainland Region (B.C.)–Climate–
Popular works. 3. Weather–Popular works.
I. Rossiter, Sean, 1946- II. Title.
III. Title: B.C. weather book.
QC985.5.B7R45 1991 551.69711 C91-091568-7

Cover photo by Ray Lum
Cover design by Barbara Hodgson
Art direction by Terri Wershler
Text design by Fiona MacGregor
Production by Elizabeth Wilson and Terri Wershler, Brighouse Press
Printed and bound in Canada

For Victor Wyatt, Jack Wells,
Father David Bauer and Gordon Craig,
all of whom played an important part in my life.
I am forever grateful.

Acknowledgements

First and foremost, it is my privilege to acknowledge the meteorological education I have received through the years from the men and women of Environment Canada with whom I deal every day. Their advice and information, often given at a moment's notice, make my forecasts on CBC-TV possible.

Certain individuals were especially helpful with this project. Gary Wells, deputy director of weather service operations, Pacific Region, Environment Canada, explained the unique weather phenomena of British Columbia. Earl Coatta, the B.C. weather office's resident climatologist, gave several interviews, read this manuscript, and was thoughtful in his suggestions. Margaret Phelan, publicist, cheerfully unearthed graphic materials from within Environment Canada's files. Many of the weather records listed in this book appeared originally in David Phillips's annual *Weather Trivia Calendars* and in his enjoyable book *The Climates of Canada.*

The experts hold no monopoly on weather wisdom in as rugged and far-flung a part of the world as we live in, but it took Lucie McNeill and the producers of *Almanac* on CBC Radio to gather much of the direct knowledge of forecasting that individuals from everywhere in B.C. have contributed to this book. I thank each of them, and all those who, unable to be heard on the program, wrote to me, often at length, with their personal weather experiences.

It was Anita Webster who laid the foundation for this book, doing much of the early first-hand research and beginning the difficult task of organizing the material. Special thanks are also due to those athletes and sports officials who graciously contributed their unique insights to the chapter on Weather and Sports. They include Jack Kelso, swim coach at UBC and an Ocean Falls aquatic champion, Grady Hall of the Vancouver Canadians, former Lions coach and sportscaster Annis Stukus, and my friends Debbie Brill and Al and Nancy Greene Raine.

Maps are an important part of any attempt to explain the weather. These maps came from many sources. Dave Phillips generously made graphics from his book available for ours. UBC Press and the UBC Geography Department were particularly forthcoming in answering our calls for help. The federal department of Energy, Mines and Resources contributed a photograph taken from their Landsat orbiter.

Photo research is a thankless task, but one that adds much to a book like this one. As always, the staffs of the Vancouver City Archives and the Provincial Archives in Victoria were eager to help and delved deeply into their treasure troves. The Historical Photographs Division of the Vancouver Public Library found images unavailable anywhere else. Environment Canada knew a good project when they saw it and opened their files. Pacific Press generously allowed us to reproduce photos that were news and have become history. Tourism B.C. found photos from every corner of the province that demonstrate why ours is "the climate with everything."

The design of the book is the work of Fiona MacGregor, who faced the challenge of assembling hundreds of visuals and pieces of text into a coherent whole. Finally, thanks to Terri Wershler and Elizabeth Wilson who kept the B.C. Weather Book alive over several years and nurtured it to its final form.

—Phil Reimer

Contents

This map has been reprinted with permission of the publisher from A.L. Farley, Atlas of British Columbia: People, Environment, and Resource Use *(Vancouver: UBC Press 1979).*

PREFACE

I didn't set out with a mission in life to be a weatherman. Weather just seems to follow me around. I was born in Winnipeg, grew up in Victoria, and now I live in Vancouver and Whistler. Natural calamities occurred everywhere I went.

I was a refugee from the Winnipeg Flood, I've been caught in offshore storms in small boats, and I've flown past thunderheads in light planes – bounced up and down 300 metres. I've even been victimized by beautiful sunny days – like so many days during the 1987 ski season. Come to think of it, I'm a weatherman in self-defence.

I'm a boater, a pilot, and a skier. (Well, I call it skiing.) All the things I do have been weather-related, so I've been a devoted student of the weather for a long time. I've had to be.

The first time I really felt the impact of weather was during the 1950 Winnipeg Flood. I was nine years old. It was about 8 o'clock in the morning and my mother sent me down to the store, which was maybe 300 metres from the house. I could see the water starting to creep up the street. I turned around, started crying, and ran home. I told my mom and dad that the water was coming up the street.

CBC TV, Vancouver

They knew it was coming, but they were surprised that it had climbed that fast during the night. As a result, we had to stay in the house, and as soon as the water was deep enough at the front door, the Army amphibious vehicles came and hauled us away.

That was also my first experience with silver linings. I got to spend the best three months of my life at a place called Virden, Manitoba, which is one of those Tom Sawyer kinds of places with a stock-car track you could sneak into and rubber-tire swings over the creeks.

The next time I saw the power of weather was my first overnight camping trip when I was in Cubs. It poured the entire time.

Being the Great White Hunter that I am, I couldn't get the fire started. (Well, *none* of us could get the fire started.) We were inside soggy tents, and were eating, as I remember, cold hot dogs – cold buns, cold weiners, and cold beans. I will never forget that. We were soaking wet, we were frozen, and it was very disillusioning that the weather could let a boy down on his first overnight camping trip.

Sometimes bad weather brings people together. It happened at the start of the 1967 Winnipeg Pan-American Games. Winnipeg went crazy for those games, and I think it was a turning point for the city. Big events do that.

We in Winnipeg were very negative about the Pan-American Games. Didn't think we could pull it off, etcetera. Then, about four months before they opened, the spirit started to build. It was very similar to what we had in Vancouver at Expo. I think we had about 10,000 volunteers. We *could* pull it off.

Prince Philip was coming to open the Games. And then, wouldn't you know it, after all the preparation, it rained the morning of the opening ceremonies. Everybody was *so* upset. They thought the games would be ruined.

And what happened was that the 25,000 people in the stands started to sort of wring out their shirts, they didn't care any more, they put down their umbrellas, and finally the athletes started marching in. And I remember a photograph of Prince Philip, deciding if everybody else was going to get into the spirit he would too. He took off his hat, got rid of the umbrella, and stood there in the rain taking the salute from all the countries, and I can still see the great big raindrops running down his regal nose and the one raindrop falling right off the end – a great picture, very vivid.

LET IT SNOW, LET IT SNOW, LET IT SNOW. Flyin' Phil takes advantage of accumulated frozen crystalline precipitation (puff, puff) at Whistler. Whistler Mountain

A comparable event was the World Cup Downhill at Whistler about four years ago. Fog rolled in. This is when it's no fun being a weather guy. In fact we'd been up there doing the weather show for three days before the World Cup. When you're the only visible weather guy in town, everybody wants to know, "Phil, what's it gonna be like? What's it gonna be like?"

Well, there was a little bit of warming coming in, so we knew there was a chance of some fog. And, sure enough, it rolled in, it rolled in, it rolled in. Lasted right through Sunday. I really wanted to disappear. Every day when there would be a press conference the people would point to the back of the room and say "Well, Phil, what do you have to say about that?"

The pressure was on. I remember being in contact with the Environment Canada people almost hourly. However, Whistler's a whole different pocket of regional weather from Vancouver. Then I got kind of brave on Sunday afternoon. I said "You know, if you can delay it by one day there's a pretty good chance."

Well, as it turned out, they could not delay by one day. The athletes had to move on. I'm eternally grateful to the airline that cancelled the charter that would have allowed them to race on the Monday and then get out of town. Because the fog was thicker than ever on Monday.

There's one area where you're really closely questioned about the weather: at the racetrack. I can't think of one other sport outside skiing where the weather plays such an important part. There are horses for courses: there are mudders, and there are horses who can run on the dry track. A horse that streaked it on a fast track could just go dead in the mud, and a bum on the dry track could go roaring away on an off-track. Weather is a great equalizer of racehorses.

If I go over to the track at 5:30 in the morning to watch the horses work, I'm bombarded by trainers and owners who say "Saturday. Whaddya think? Whaddya think?"

LET IT SHOW, LET IT SHOW, LET IT SHOW. Weather broadcasting in Winnipeg in the old days . . . and no, they didn't make me wear that outfit, that's Rocket Reimer, just in from a charity hockey game. CKY TV, Winnipeg

Because you have to enter about three days ahead of time for races, they're always curious as to how the weather is going to turn up that particular day. So am I. I've owned a dozen or so horses, and it's really hard to tell whether or not you should enter your horse. Weekends are as much of a gamble for me as for anyone else.

About 12 years ago I was doing boating and fishing reports out on the water for a radio station. It gave me a great appreciation of the various conditions. I would see all the charts on Thursday, Friday and Saturday morning, and I would see how it related to conditions on Georgia Strait, Strait of Juan de Fuca and Howe Sound. It was phenomenally interesting in that it never, ever ran true to pattern.

I remember one day we had a Gale Warning verging on a Storm Warning and the seas were pitching, and there I was bouncing along in about a two-metre sea trying to hold the boat together. I was broadcasting into the microphone, "Don't come out. It's very very bad. There's no shelter anywhere. Stay in, this is not the day you should be out there."

Then I looked around and realized, *I'm the only guy on the water!*

That's when it hit me. I thought, *Oh oh, time to take my own advice.*

Doing the weather from the roof of the CBC: Believe me, it wasn't my idea. My boss's inspiration was that the weatherman has always done his report from the comfort of the studio. He always wanted to stick me outside for that first minute, so we could do battle with the elements.

We've got a little shed up there where we protect our equipment. The doors have been ripped off by storm-force winds. Umbrellas have gone flying off the roof. I've worn parkas, toques, face-masks and everything else up in that frozen corner of the CBC. You're about five stories off the ground and as a result you get the full force of the weather.

So I *do* get outside, *every* night – for one minute – to get the full effects of the weather on the Lower Mainland. It's not as if I haven't had any personal experience with what the weather can do to you. Major floods, camping in the rain, being in an offshore gale, airborne in instrument-flying weather, running my speed horses in mud – you'd think a weatherman could avoid these little inconveniences, wouldn't you?

Not me. I'm like one of the cobbler's children, right? They're the ones who go barefoot.

WEATHER AROUND THE PROVINCE

We know British Columbia is unique. "Nowhere in the world do trees grow so big, or rivers run so fast, or valleys produce such quantities of fruit, or mountain peaks soar to such heights from sea level" as in our corner of the world, Timothy Egan writes in *The Good Rain*.

All these blessings are causes or effects of our climate. As impressive as B.C.'s mountains and valleys, rivers and deserts, hot springs and glaciers are, the weather they produce is even more remarkable. Much of the time, in much of British Columbia, the weather is mild. But it can run to sudden and malevolent extremes.

Our coastline is wetter than anywhere else on the top third of the globe. The Interior is one of the driest parts of Canada. British Columbia as a whole gets more snow than anywhere else in North America, but our ocean ports never freeze. Just inland from those ports are sprawling glaciers that never thaw. David Phillips of Environment Canada calls ours "the climate with everything."

B.C. Weather Records

Highest temperature	Lytton, Lillooet	44.4°C	July 16, 1941
Most consecutive hot days (above 32°C)	Oliver, Hedley	31 days	starting July 14, 1971
Lowest temperature	Smith River	-58.9°C	Jan. 31, 1947
Most consecutive cold days (below -18°C)	Smith River	85	starting Nov. 30, 1968
Lowest temperature with wind chill	Old Glory Mountain	-69°C	Dec. 15, 1964
Longest frost-free period	Victoria	685 days	1925-26
Most precipitation in 24 hours	Ucluelet	489.2 mm	Oct. 6, 1967
Most precipitation in 1 month	Swanson Bay	2235.5 mm	Nov. 1917
Most precipitation in 1 year	Henderson Lake	8122.4 mm	1931
Highest average annual precipitation	Henderson Lake	6655 mm	
Most wet days	Langara	300 days	1939
Most consecutive days with precipitation	River Jordan	55 days	
Most consecutive days without precipitation	Kingsgate	114 days	
Most snow in 1 season	Revelstoke (Mt. Copeland)	2447 cm	1971-72
Most snow in 1 month	Haines	535.9 cm	Dec. 1959
Most snow in 1 day	Lakelse Lake	118.1 cm	Jan. 17, 1974
Highest average annual snow	Glacier (Mt. Fidelity)	1433 cm	
Most foggy days	Old Glory Mountain	254	1964
Highest average number fog days	Cape St. James	110	
Lowest average number fog days	Penticton	1-4	
Highest recorded sun	Victoria	2426 hours	1970
Highest average sun	Cranbrook	2244 hours	
Least average sun	Stewart	949 hours	
Highest wind	Bonilla Island	143 km/h	Feb. 20, 1974
Most days with gale force winds	Cape St. James	120 days	

Weather Records

BC Weather Records

This base map has been reprinted with permission of the publisher from A.L. Farley, Atlas of British Columbia: People, Environment, and Resource Use *(Vancouver: UBC Press 1979). Copyright University of British Columbia Press. All rights reserved.*

While Vancouver can record the heaviest rainfall of any Canadian city, Lillooet can be the hottest, driest place in Canada. Vancouver and Lillooet are barely 150 km apart as the crow flies, but mountain ranges between them put them in different worlds climatically. British Columbia has dozens of these microclimates.

Ocean Falls, for example, is the wettest populated place in Canada. Prince Rupert is wet too, but in a different way. It has the lowest average number of days of sunshine of any city in the country: it is the nation's drizzle capital. Kamloops, on the other hand, is the driest, hottest city in Canada.

Wettest, driest. Warmest, snowiest. Highest, lowest. We get a lot of weather in British Columbia.

With extremely wet and dry climates like those of Prince Rupert and Kamloops, it is no wonder B.C. holds so many weather records. We hold most of Canada's maximum rainfall records, and all the records for most and least snowfall. British Columbia also enjoys the country's highest average daily and annual temperatures, the greatest annual average temperature range, and Canada's longest frost-free period. Some parts of coastal B.C. enjoy as many as 220 frost-free days – much longer than anywhere else in Canada – and all of the B.C. coastline is ice free year round.

The most consistently warm place in Canada is Sumas Canal (60 km east of Vancouver), where the annual average temperature is 10.7°C. This is partly because the city of Vancouver acts as a moderating force on weather in the Fraser Valley, warming the west wind and absorbing its moisture before air is funnelled down the Fraser River trench.

The lower Fraser was known to freeze regularly during our grandparents' lifetimes. A

From one extreme to the other. The Walachin area near Kamloops is Canada's only desert. Cedar Valley, near Bella Coola, is rainforest. Province of British Columbia

new bridge between Lulu and Sea Islands collapsed under pressure from ice floes in 1890. There was ice on the Fraser during Vancouver's worst winter storm in January, 1935 – enough to close sawmills and resist attempts to dynamite passageways for boats. But now heat and air pollution from increasing urbanization on the Lower Mainland seldom allow the mighty Fraser to freeze.

Snowfall Records

B.C. holds all Canadian snowfall records:

Most in one day: 118.1 cm, Lakelse Lake, January 17, 1974. (Lakelse Lake is south of Terrace and is the Tsimshian Indian word for "fresh water mussel.") *Most in one month:* 535.9 cm, Haines, December 1959. (The Haines weather station was in the extreme NW corner of the province.) *Most in one season*: 2447 cm, Revelstoke / Mt. Copeland, 1971-72. (The elevation at the weather station is 1847 m.) *Greatest average annual:* 1433 cm, Glacier, Mt. Fidelity. (Glacier is in B.C.'s extreme SE corner. The elevation at weather station is 1875 m.)

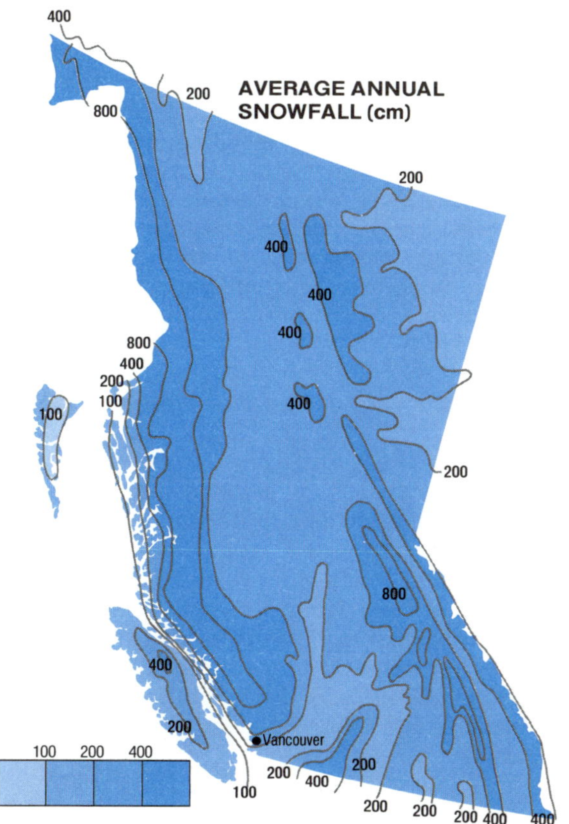

The Climates of Canada. *David Phillips, Environment Canada, 1990*

Half the precipitation around Enderby, southeast of Salmon Arm, falls as snow. D. Clemson Armstrong, photo 33829, Vancouver Public Library

Precipitation Records

Most precipitation in one year: 8122.4 mm, Henderson Lake, 1931. *Most in one month:* 2235.5 mm, Swanson Bay, November 1917. (Swanson Bay is on the mainland coast across from the Queen Charlottes; it is named for Capt. John Swanson of the Hudson's Bay Company maritime service, who commanded, among other vessels, the S.S. *Beaver*.) *Most in one day:* 489.2 mm, Ucluelet, October 6, 1967. (Ucluelet is on the west coast of Vancouver Island. It is from the Nootka Indian word meaning "people of the sheltered bay.")

Highest average annual: 6655 mm, Henderson Lake (near Port Alberni). *Lowest average annual:* 205.6 mm, Ashcroft.

Hoarfrost is frozen water vapour. Here, water vapour given off by trees overnight is flash-frozen, forming a natural art deco gateway in the forest. D. Clemson Armstrong, photo 33818, Vancouver Public Library

Longest wet spell: 300 days, Langara, 1939 (at the northern end of the Queen Charlottes). *Longest wet spell of any major city in Canada:* 33 days, Victoria, starting April 19, 1986. (Vancouver is next at 29 days starting January 6, 1953.)

Wet Spots

Henderson Lake may or may not be the wettest place in Canada, inhabited or uninhabited. It is located at the end of a funnel-shaped valley, which is at the end of an arm of Barkley Sound on the outer coast of Vancouver Island. Warm, moist winds from the Pacific are concentrated as they rush toward narrow Alberni Inlet and spill over the inlet's canyon-like walls. Henderson Lake is no longer inhabited by even the single individual who, during the 1920s and early '30s, collected the most rainwater of any weather station volunteer in the country.

Most weather stations are operated by volunteers, and there hasn't been one living at remote Henderson Lake since 1936. This raises the question of whether Henderson Lake's record rainfalls have been exceeded in some equally inaccessible spot.

There are at least 550 weather recording stations in B.C., points out Earl Coatta, Environment Canada's chief climatologist. He is always looking for more volunteers. Oddly enough, there are only two in Vancouver – partly because so many buildings eliminate possible nearby sites – and none in New Westminster.

"Who knows," Coatta asks, "what happens at places where we *don't* have rain gauges?"

Ocean Falls, the site of a pulp and paper mill from 1909 to 1980, averages 4386 mm of precipitation per year. It is generally considered to be Canada's wettest inhabited place, although it is now more a village than a town, with about one-tenth of its peak population of 3000. Ocean Falls is perfectly situated to be Canada's rain capital: amid inlets, lakes and channels, between the moist Queen Charlotte Islands and a stretch of the north Coast Mountains with peaks running from 2500 to 3500 metres.

Ucluelet holds the B.C. record for most precipitation in 24 hours. But this is proof that Ucluelet does get the occasional sunny day. Province of British Columbia

Sunshine Records

Least average annual: 949 hours, Stewart (one-quarter of the possible total). *Highest average annual:* 2244 hours, Cranbrook. *Most sunshine on record:* 2426 hours, Victoria, 1970.

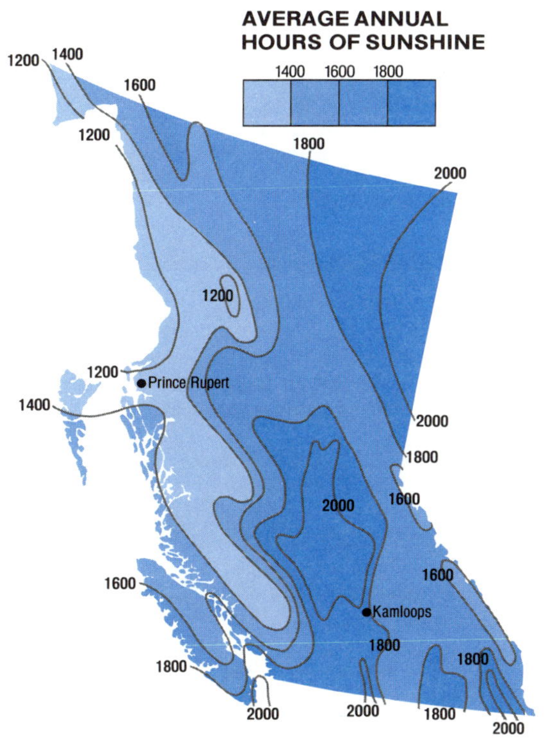

The Climates of Canada. *David Phillips, Environment Canada, 1990*

Temperature Records

Hottest city in Canada: Kamloops, 24 days, 1958. (Kamloops has the most very hot days – 35°C or more – and the most such days on average, 8.)

Hottest day in B.C: July 16, 1941, Lillooet and Lytton, 44.4°C. *Coldest day in B.C:* January 31, 1947, Smith River, -58.9°C.

Longest frost-free period: 685 days, Victoria, 1925-26.

And We Think We Get Rain!

While coastal British Columbians often refer to the wet season as "the monsoons," the term is not even symbolically apt. The wettest place in the world, Mount Waialeale, Hawaii, receives 11,680 mm annually, almost three times the rainfall of Ocean Falls.

But the intensity of rainfall in those wet equatorial regions, such as the South China Sea and the eastern Bay of Bengal, where real monsoon rainstorms rage, can bring life to a halt. The world record for rainfall over one year was set at Cherrapunji, India, where, from August 1860 to July 1861, 26,461 mm of rain – or *87 feet* – fell.

The area just outside Kamloops has one of Canada's driest climates. Province of British Columbia

Fog Records

Most foggy days: 254, Old Glory Mountain, 1964. (At Old Glory the weather station is at 2347 m.)

Highest average number of foggy days: 110 days, Cape St. James (on the south tip of Queen Charlotte Islands). *Lowest average number of foggy days:* 1-4 per year, Penticton.

Wind Records

Highest wind speed: 143 km/h, Bonilla Island, February 20, 1974. (Bonilla Island is just south of Prince Rupert.)

Highest average number of days with gale-force winds: 120 days, Cape St. James.

Speaking of wind . . .

The term squamish winds has become a generic term for outflow air currents: winds that blow out of a valley or channel, often at very high speeds, up to 100 km/h. Howe Sound is a north-south channel that can serve as an outlet for cold arctic air that often sits over the Interior in winter. In Howe Sound the speed of the winds is exaggerated by the tightness of the channel. The waters off the town of Squamish are known as the best windsurfing location in B.C. because of the frequency and magnitude of these winds. (By the way, Howe Sound was named by Captain Vancouver after Admiral the Right Honourable Richard Scrope, Earl Howe – known affectionately to his sailors as "Black Dick" because of his fondness for battle.)

Because squamish winds can be a marine hazard, a special weather buoy was installed in June 1987 on the east side of Gambier

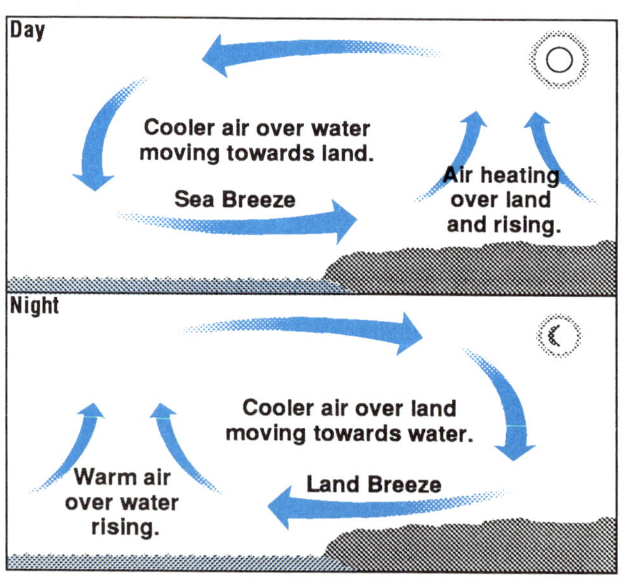

On warm days, when prevailing winds are light, air over land heats and rises. Cooler air from over the water moves in to take its place, creating a sea breeze. When a sea breeze is funnelled though an inlet, wind speeds can reach up to 30 knots. In evening, when the land cools, the direction of the air flow is reversed. Land breezes are generally not as strong as sea breezes. Environment Canada

The Peace River district – a little corner of the prairies in British Columbia. Province of British Columbia

Island, near the mouth of Howe Sound. It transmits data hourly via satellite to the Pacific Weather Centre in Vancouver.

Geography and Weather

"The first almighty fact about British Columbia," the late naturalist Roderick Haig-Brown wrote, "is mountains."

Three-quarters of B.C. is mountains. Six mountain ranges run diagonally up and down the Pacific Coast and along the Alberta border. The Interior Plateau stretches in-between. Finally, tucked up in the northeast corner of the province, the Peace River district, is part of the Great Plains region that links B.C. with the rest of Canada. Each of these regions has its own climate.

For a fisherman like Haig-Brown, the second almighty fact about B.C. would have been water. A newcomer to the Lower Mainland is confronted by five bodies of water emptying into Georgia Strait from North Vancouver to White Rock. This pattern of convoluted coastline, with inlets, fjords and islands, only becomes more complicated farther north. If straightened out, the B.C. coast would be 7000 km long, but as the crow flies it is only 700 km.

The most powerful network of river systems on the North American continent is fed by the high glacier-capped mountains of the Selkirk, Purcell, and Monashee ranges of the Rockies. The deep snowfields of these majestic ranges feed the Thompson, Columbia, and Fraser rivers that eat their way through deep rock canyons etched out of parched valleys of sagebrush and ponderosa pine, to the Pacific.

Any more than 2000 mm of rain per year is extraordinary anywhere within the earth's temperate zones. B.C.'s long, twisting coast-

This base map has been reprinted with permission of the publisher from A.L. Farley, Atlas of British Columbia: People, Environment, and Resource Use *(Vancouver: UBC Press 1979). Copyright University of British Columbia Press. All rights reserved.*

Landsat Mosaic of British Columbia

This aerial photograph is copyright 1979 by Her Majesty the Queen in Right of Canada, reproduced from the collection of the National Air Photo Library with permission of Energy, Mines and Resources Canada.

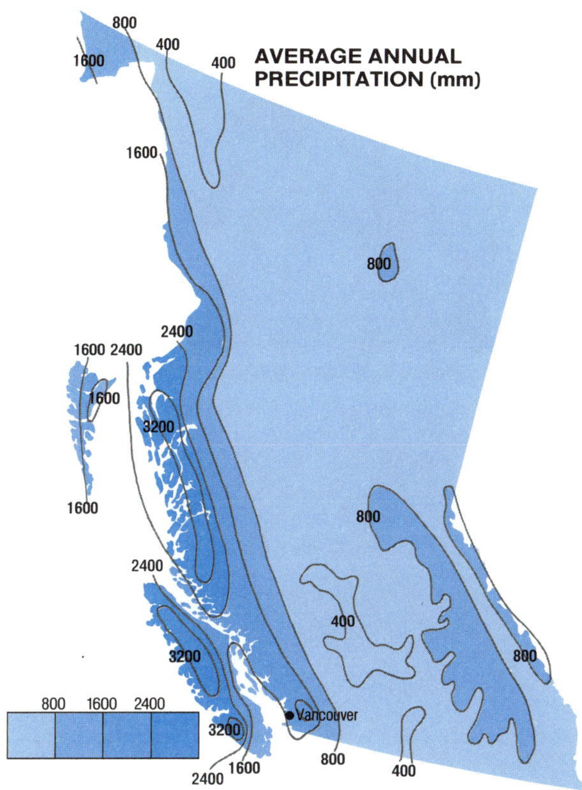

The Climates of Canada, *David Phillips, Environment Canada, 1990*

line is the only part of the northern hemisphere's temperate zone where rainfall exceeds 2500 mm per year. Parts of the B.C.

This base map has been reprinted with permission of the publisher from A.L. Farley, Atlas of British Columbia: People, Environment, and Resource Use *(Vancouver: UBC Press 1979). Copyright University of British Columbia Press. All rights reserved.*

coast, such as the Queen Charlotte Islands, the northern tip of Vancouver Island, and the rugged coastline in-between, often receive much more than that.

Yet parts of B.C.'s Interior are, for all intents and purposes, desert or arid scrubland, suitable only for limited grazing. The mountains that cover three-quarters of B.C. create microclimates of their own: desert to lush valley to glacier. Similar climates exist in Chile and the South Island of New Zealand, and for the same reason: immovable objects – row upon row of mountains – are confronted by the irresistible force of winds blowing from the ocean.

Climate Zones

Just as the elements that shape B.C.'s weather can be refined down to two – mountains and water – so can its climatic zones – Coastal and Interior. Loosely speaking, B.C. has wet and dry climatic zones. The Coast is wet, the Interior dry. A third climatic zone, northeastern B.C.'s Peace River region, shares its climate with much of the rest of the country. Also, pockets of a warm, dry Mediterranean-like climate are found on the Gulf Islands, the Saanich Peninsula and around Qualicum.

Rain Shadow

Above the water and rock, in the tumbling mirth of the winds, all of our weather hurdles mountains or whistles through valleys and passes. It is generated by air masses over the North Pacific. These air masses move east as part of the general movement of the northern hemisphere's winds. This moist Pacific air rises over the west faces of the Olympic, Vancouver Island, Coast, and Cascade mountains, cooling as it climbs. The air condenses its moisture into clouds that drape the western slopes in fog and rain, watering the coastal rain forests.

These west winds create an entirely differ-

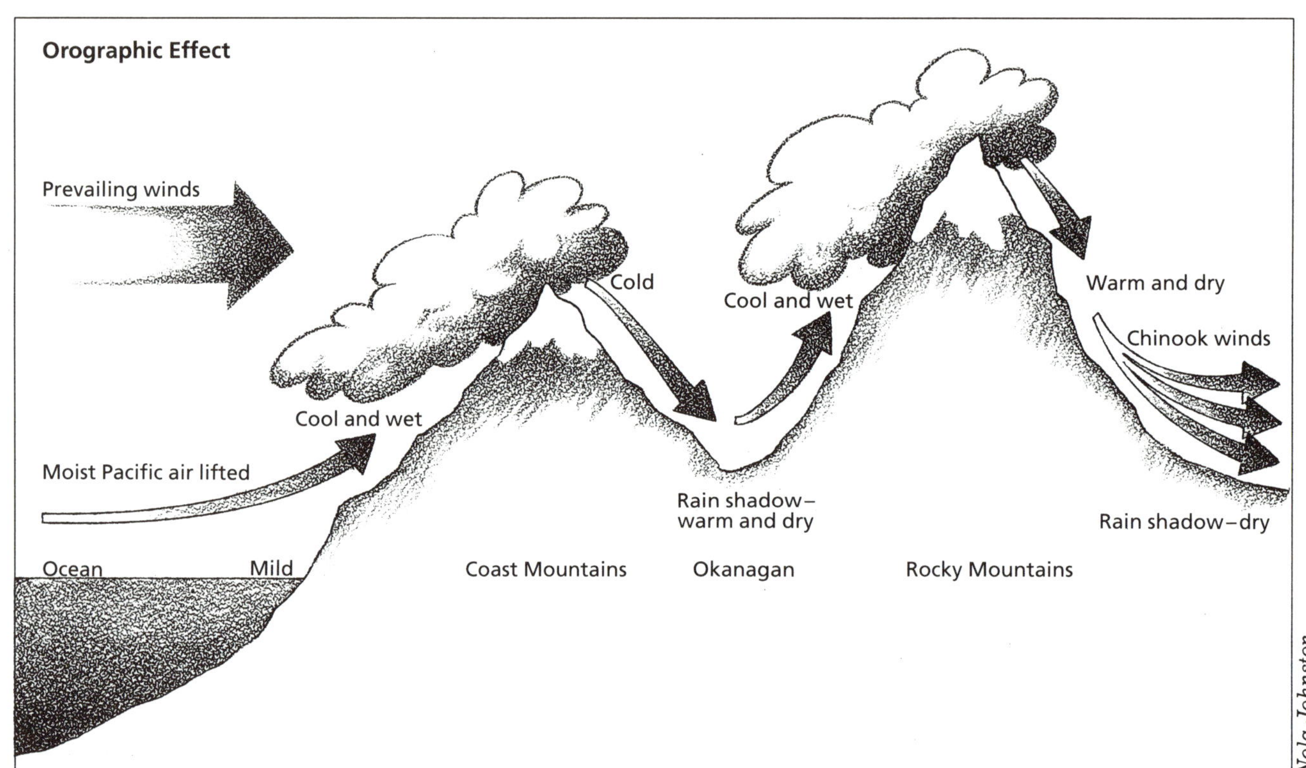

ent climate as they descend eastward, down the other side, gathering warmth. Suddenly, as air moves over the mountain ridge, the lush vegetation of the western, windward side – fir, hemlock and cedar, dripping with moss and encrusted with exotic fungi, towering over a floor carpeted in luxuriant ferns – turns to desert. The same wind that turns rising mist to downpour on one side, loses its vapour and actually sucks moisture from slopes on the other side.

This is called the Orographic Effect, or rain shadow (from the Greek *oros* or mountain). More than any other weather principle, the rain shadow explains the extremes of climate felt in locations close to each other. Victoria, the Saanich Peninsula and the Gulf Islands, with the driest climate on the southwest coast (some call it Mediterranean) climate, lie in the rain shadow of the sodden Olympic Mountains of Washington State.

These winds warmed and dried out by passage over mountains are known in Canada by the Indian name of chinooks, or snow-eaters. They can evaporate snow at rate of two-thirds of a metre a day. Extreme chinooks blow most often in southern Alberta, after having passed over several southeastern B.C. ranges, but they also occasionally warm Fort Nelson, in the Peace River district, after passing over the Rockies.

Orographic Effect or Rain Shadow

An illustration of the rain shadow effect is the average annual precipitation rates for Prince Rupert (3000 mm/yr) compared to Terrace (1500 mm) and Smithers (450 mm). Terrace, about 140 km inland from Prince Rupert, is fairly wet. Then Smithers, 60 km farther inland, is suddenly almost arid. The difference is that Prince Rupert and Terrace are linked climatically by the widest part of the Skeena River and its canyon. Terrace and Smithers, however, are separated by mountains and lie in different climatic zones. Terrace is within the Hazelton Range of the Coast Mountains, while Smithers is on the east side of the mountains in the dry Interior Plateau.

National Climate Severity Index

13	Victoria
18	Vancouver
34	Calgary
35	Toronto
37	Edmonton
37	Windsor
41	London
42	Saskatoon
43	Ottawa
43	Halifax
44	Montreal
47	Regina
48	Charlottetown
48	Saint John
51	Winnipeg
52	Quebec City
56	St. John's

Provincial Climate Severity Index

13	Victoria
16	Penticton
18	Vancouver
20	Kamloops
21	Abbotsford
22	Comox
24	Cranbrook
26	Williams Lake
28	Hope
28	Tofino
29	Castlegar
30	Port Hardy
30	Sandspit
32	Quesnel
34	Prince Rupert
35	Smithers
38	Prince George
44	Fort St. John
46	Terrace
47	Fort Nelson

Yes, that's Victoria. A soldier struggles through a waist-high snow bank on Government Street, February 1916. Photo HP 88779 British Columbia Archives

Climate Severity Index

Environment Canada's Climate Severity Index rates Victoria first among Canadian cities for liveable weather. Each number on the index is a penalty-point awarded for uncomfortably extreme temperatures, humidity, snow and rainfall, and the likelihood of weather-related disasters. As in golf, the higher your score, the worse you are doing. Victoria holds B.C.'s records for the most hours of sunshine in a year, the longest frost-free period (and, alas, the longest wet spell for a major Canadian city: 33 days starting April 19, 1986).

But, although the southern Strait of Georgia may fall below the 49th parallel, it is not quite the banana belt. Winter has not been

Victoria's lone snowplow makes little headway through wet, heavy snow after the storm of 1916. Photo HP68848, British Columbia Archives

completely eliminated. Victoria has had some humdinger winters – 1915-16 for example. Victoria's worst winter for snowfall was something of a gift from Vancouver. There, subfreezing temperatures had arrived a few days after Christmas 1915, and by the end of January, 155 cm of snow had fallen on the Lower Mainland. With 90 cm of its own snow during the same period, Victoria thought the worst was over.

Nothing doing. The City of Gardens woke up February 2 to find everything – early bulbs, green grass – covered in waist-deep snow. And it kept on coming: 116 cm more during February. Drifts of 175 cm stopped the Esquimalt & Nanaimo Railway in its tracks. Public transit was paralyzed, schools closed, and soldiers were reduced to searching for firewood on beaches because of the lack of fuel. The roof of the mess hall at Willow Camp collapsed under the snow. Only one snow plow was available; it piled snow seven feet high on each side of the thoroughfares it cleared. Mechanized fire-fighting equipment was useless; only horse-drawn vehicles could get to fires. Once there, they had to find the hydrants, which were covered with several feet of snow. Such was the novelty of the snow that someone actually calculated that the storm at the beginning of February dropped 1.4 million tonnes on B.C.'s capital.

Anatomy of a Severe Winter Storm

A high-pressure system, called the Pacific, or Hawaiian High, brings generally dry weather from mid-Pacific, while the brooding, wet Aleutian Low lies in ambush in the Gulf of Alaska. These two offshore weather systems are constantly fighting it out to dominate B.C.'s weather.

The Aleutian Low is a permanent presence in the Gulf of Alaska, generated by the meeting of cold northern air and warmer air from the south and east. The Low forms where the air masses meet, and, by developing a low-pressure system's typical counterclockwise air currents, governs the direction of the mainly southerly winds farther down the coast. These winds can attain gale or storm-force velocity.

The movement of storms that develop out in the Pacific, such as 1962's Typhoon Freda, are directed by these winds north and east along the coast, often spinning remnant storms off to batter outer Vancouver Island or the Queen Charlottes. They swing east along the front, north offshore along the coast, and eventually west along the Alaska coast, giving television weather forecast watchers the spiral pattern of clouds that appear on satellite pictures. Meteorologists call the powerful storms that spin off the edges of these rotary systems and smash the coasts "marine bombs."

The term bomb literally describes the way the air pressure plummets as these storms approach British Columbia from off the Oregon or California coasts, as the remnants of Freda did, gathering strength as they move east. The counter-clockwise winds governed by the Aleutian Low can kick more cold air into the backs of these storms, increasing their severity.

Their winds first batter the outer coast of Vancouver Island—Nootka Sound, on the island's north coast, is known to sailors and fishermen as the graveyard of the North Pacific. They are preceded by waves of 8 or 9 metres moving north toward the Queen Charlottes and Hecate Strait. Once the storm itself has continued north to Alaska, it leaves its finishing kick: heavy swells along the south coast up to 12 hours after the storm has passed.

What to Watch for as a Front Approaches
This is a sequence of weather signs observed at Cape St. James, the south end of the Queen Charlotte Islands. The pattern gives six to eight hours' warning of gale force winds with the front approaching the coast at 35-40 knots.

21 hours	Winds light westerly, scattered clouds, barometer rising slowly. Increasing cirrus, stratocirrus provide early warning of approaching front.
17 hours	Cirrus widespread, wind shift light SE.
15 hours	Overcast, thickening cirrostratus, barometer begins to fall at 1 mb/h. Later, clouds lower to altostratus, winds increase to SE 10-15 knots: good warning of impending storm.
11 hours	Heavy overcast, cloud lower, rain begins, winds increase to SE 18-20 knots. Pressures fall more rapidly.
5 hours	Winds to gale force S-SE. Visibility lowered to 5 km in rain and fog, pressure falling 1.5-2.0 mb/h. Frontal S-SE gales continue for 5-6 hours. Near front, winds reach gusts 50-60 knots. Visibility 2.5 km, 1 km at front. Pressure falls 3 mb/h until front passes. After passage winds shift to SW 20-25 knots, little change next 12 hours, widely scattered showers, barometer rises 1 mb/h.

– from *Marine Weather Hazards Along the British Columbia Coast.*

This marine weather hazards manual is dedicated to the memory of the five fishermen who were lost in the severe storm of October 7-12, 1984 off Nootka Sound. During that storm many coastal communities registered 100 mm rain in 24 hours. On October 11, gale-force winds pounded northwest Vancouver Island, the Queen Charlottes, and the north coast of B.C. Winds measured at Cape St. James reached hurricane force at 120 km/h with gusts to 160. Ten-metre waves capsized eight fishboats.

It may be true that everybody talks about the weather, but there *are* some people who have done something about it. Anyone who has moved to the west coast has done more than just gripe about the weather.

In moving to Vancouver we feel, deep down, that we have taken the weather into our own hands. We have saved ourselves from the worst weather this country has to offer. We no longer define ourselves as many Canadians do – in terms of survival. We do better than survive. We enjoy ourselves.

In Vancouver we see ourselves living outdoors. All of us would rather be sailing – or rock-climbing, driving with the top down, or just sitting on a log, watching the sun go down. We work so we can play. One sign of a long-term Vancouver resident is that he – or, even more likely, she – will ignore precipitation until it starts raining cats and dogs. Women love rain; they find getting wet romantic.

In this spirit of ac-cen-tchuat-ing the positive, even the meteorologists at Environment Canada often make it sound better than it is. When, for example, has the Weather Office actually come right out and predicted "Days and Days of Heavy Rain?" Why does "intermittent showers" usually turn out to be steady rain? Why does "rain" – when you hear that word, *look out* – often mean a wind-driven downpour?

The meteorologists are good sports about their levels-of-precipitation forecasts, which they claim to be accurate about half the time. For 24-hour forecasts of temperatures, they are right 95 percent of the time, and on

Vancouver: if you don't like the weather, wait five minutes. Downtown cloudy; West End sunny; Kitsilano overcast.
Larry Wolfson

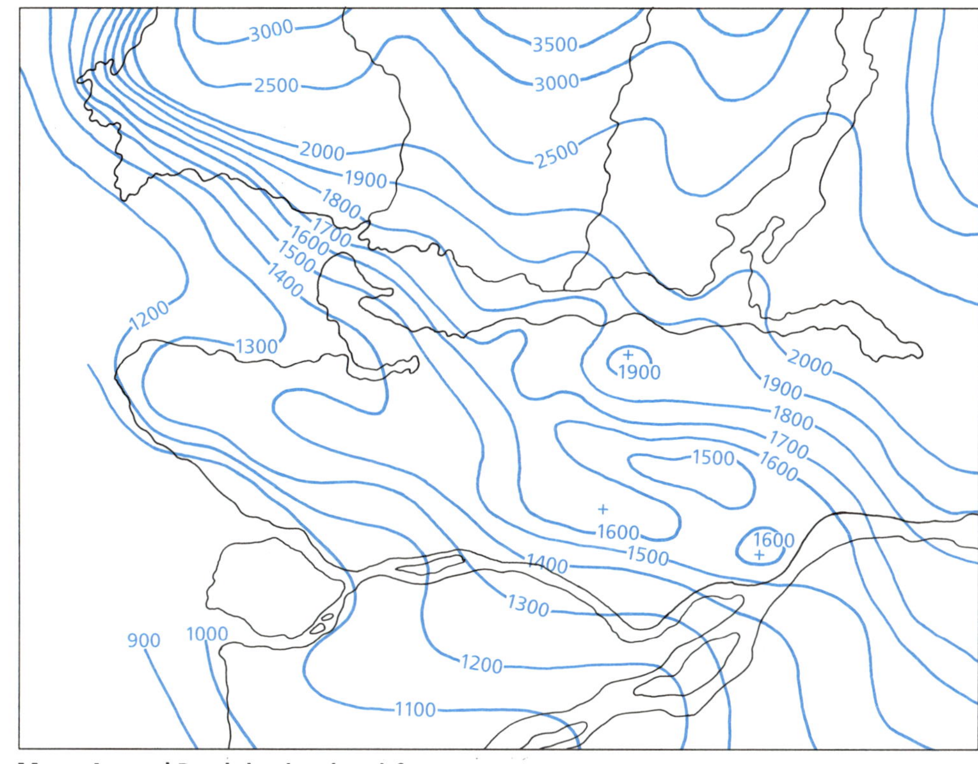

Mean Annual Precipitation (mm) for Greater Vancouver

The Climate of Vancouver, *Hay and Oke, UBC Geography Department, 1976*

whether or not there will be precipitation at all, their rate of accuracy is an impressive 80 percent. As for *how much* rain, your guess is often as good as anyone else's.

"I've been forecasting all across Canada," says Gary Wells, deputy director of weather service operations for the Environment Canada's Pacific Region. "My feeling is the west coast is still the most difficult (to predict the weather), more challenging than elsewhere in the country."

Microclimates

One of the first weather observations newcomers to Vancouver make is that the clouds seem to gather around the North Shore mountains and thin out as you move south. More than three times as much rain falls on Hollyburn, Grouse and Seymour as falls on Richmond (up to 3000 mm vs. 1100 mm or so). At The Lions, back in the mountain watershed, it is estimated that annual rainfalls of 5000 mm are common. One hundred millimetres of additional rainfall per 100 m of elevation is a good rule-of-thumb. In Vancouver, more rain is the price you pay for a panoramic view. Most of us have no idea how gloomy and dispiriting life in the British Properties can be.

"Some people," Wells says, "view mountains as a high wall. They deflect weather systems up and down. For example, it could be raining in the North Shore mountains and sunny in Tsawwassen. Those climates are different, and mountains are the primary reason for it."

Those two microclimates are so different because of their opposite relationships to mountains. North and West Vancouver are on the windward slopes of the North Shore mountains. Clouds gather there, are driven upward, get cooler with altitude, and their water vapor condenses in the form of rain or snow. Tsawwassen is on the opposite, or leeward side of the Olympic Mountains of Washington State. Tsawwassen is in the rain shadow of the Olympics: clouds meeting the Olympics have been drained on the west slopes and so clear, dry air reaches Tsawwassen.

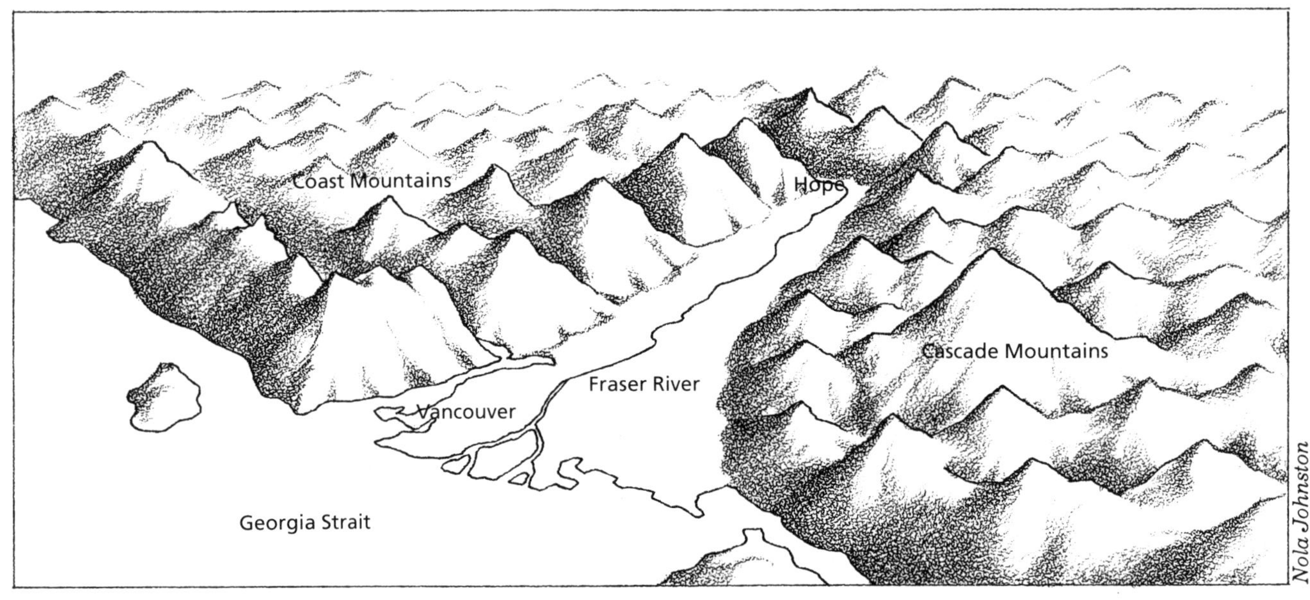

River delta, inlet, and looming mountains – the Lower Mainland's extremes of topography are responsible for its unique weather. Environment Canada

How We Change Weather

The simple fact that we live here has an effect on our weather. It is warmer in the air above roads, buildings, and concentrations of people. The temperature dips by a degree or two Celsius over such undeveloped areas as Stanley Park, Queen Elizabeth Park, and Langara Golf Course, compared with, say, the intersection of Georgia and Burrard. There is, believe it or not, a diagonal "warm arm along Kingsway," as one meteorology text puts it.

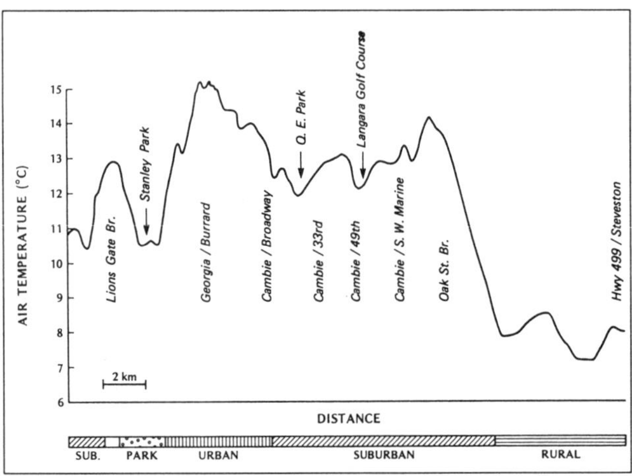

Effects of urbanization: Concrete heats the air above it, parkland creates columns of cooler air in the atmosphere. (Readings taken at 12:30 AM Sept. 15, 1973, moving from the Fraser Delta to West Vancouver via Downtown.) The Climate of Vancouver, *Hay and Oke, UBC Geography Department, 1976*

With its mixture of urbanization and wilderness, the North Shore shows this effect best, with a core of heat above the foot of Lonsdale Avenue while the stream beds of the Capilano and Seymour rivers and Lynn Creek keep the air above them cold. As housing advances up Hollyburn, Grouse and Seymour, we can expect to see the scenic mountaintop snowcap recede.

There is never any shortage of opinion that air pollution is getting worse over any major city. In Vancouver, though, there is good – if old – news: *visible* pollution has declined to the point where Vancouver International Airport is recording one-quarter to one-third the number of foggy days we had in the 1940s. Much of the 90 days of fog that Vancouver used to get consisted of water vapor condensing around airborne particles from coal, wood and sawdust-burning furnaces in homes and industry. The sawmills that ringed the south shore of False Creek burned off sawdust in "teepee" furnaces until the 1960s. The fog we still experience 20-30 days a year is relatively pure and white, if just as hard to see through.

Vancouver used to have more fog – from 90 days a year in the 1940s to just 20 or 30 days a year now. Deni Eagland, The Vancouver Sun

Best Climate, Worst Weather?

So the best and worst things about living in Vancouver are the weather. When it's good, it's great. You hate to have someone you care for depart without seeing the city on one of those sensationally clear, sharp-focus days when the mountains look close enough to touch, when English Bay is white with sails, and there are just enough clouds for a Technicolor sunset. Those days can come at any time, even February. They come as welcome surprises; gifts from above. They affirm the decisions so many of us made either to move to Vancouver or to stay here.

To easterners, weather is something that afflicts; something to be coped with, more inevitable than death or taxes. Easterners hunker down for winter and sweat out summer. While they endure weather, on the coast we live in it. Weather is important to us, mainly because we're going to be out in it anyway. It was in B.C. that houses with walls of glass, to bring the outdoors inside, first appeared in Canada. Anywhere else in Canada, why would anyone want to bring the environment indoors?

Here's how hot and cold it can get. In terms of all-time records, Regina is the worst: On New Year's Day, 1885, Regina hit -50°; on July 5, 1937, 43.3°, a variation of 93°C.

Compare that to a 51°C variation in Vancouver, where the coldest recorded temperature was -18°C on January 15, 1950, and repeated December 29, 1968. The highest temperature ever recorded at Vancouver International Airport was 33.3°C, on August 9, 1960 – and, hey, that's hot enough!

Although we do occasionally lose faith, the record shows that Vancouver has a history of rising to the occasion, weather-wise. We may have the most unpredictable weather on the continent, but when there's something at stake the skies shape up.

When Captain George Vancouver shows up unexpectedly in Burrard Inlet, when Roger Bannister passes John Landy at the finish of the Miracle Mile, or when Expo 86 starts to look like a washout, summer suddenly makes its appearance.

Although the weather records for the noon hour of June 13, 1792, are incomplete – we only started keeping track in 1898 – the painting of Captain Vancouver's pair of longboats entering "Burrard's Canal" shows a limp Royal Navy ensign, sunshine, and the tops of the North Shore mountains as clear as day. A much more reliable indication, and one the captain wisely dwells upon in his diary, is the fact that the natives were friendly. They didn't have to apologize for the weather. Thank heaven: Sir Francis Drake encountered "thicke mists and most stinking fogges" along the Pacific coast in 1579 and sailed home in disgust. If Captain Vancouver had encountered the same conditions, there might not be one-and-a-half million of us living on the Lower Mainland today.

Captain Vancouver's appearance was not the only local first to be aided by the weather. Charles Saunders made the first parachute jump in Canada on May 24, 1912, a day when there were light winds, no precipitation, and it was 21°C in Vancouver. When the first Trans-Canada Air Lines passenger flight took off, in a brightly-polished Lockheed Model 10, from Sea Island bound for Seattle, conditions were perfect: moderate winds, temperature 22°C, and clear skies.

Winds were only 9 km/h outside the brand-new Empire Stadium, and reduced to a few eddies inside on August 7, 1954, as John Landy looked over his shoulder a few strides from the end of the Miracle Mile and Roger Bannister won by passing him on his blind side. Both men ran sub-four-minute miles.

The 1983 Grey Cup, played November 27 in Vancouver, was one of the few Canadian Football League championship games not remembered as a Mud or Fog Bowl. Winds were almost non-existent that day, at 3 km/h, there was not the slightest chance of precipitation, and the temperature was 21°C. Of course, that was also the first Grey Cup played indoors, at B.C. Place Stadium. (Argos 18, B.C. Lions 17.)

Hands up, everyone who told visiting relatives how embarrassed you were about the rotten, miserable weather we had during the first couple of months of Expo 86. Right up to July 17: unseasonable cold, unremitting overcast skies, rain that sometimes seemed horizontal, a freezing South Seas pavilion, a constantly dripping Swatch Watch.

Then, from July 17 to September 9, there was no rain. No rain what-so-ever! No rain for

Why One Man Moved to Vancouver

(He moved from Ottawa. What else do you need to know?)

Ottawa is the coldest capital city in the world: colder on average than Moscow, Helsinki, Oslo, and a whole lot colder than Reykjavik. Ottawa summers are no screaming hell either.

I survived the two winters from late 1970 to early 1972, which set consecutive records for snowfall in Ottawa. I worked for *The Ottawa Citizen* for most of those two winters, and the most interesting assignments were winter war stories: many of them brutal crimes brought on by cabin fever. By Christmas 1971 it was obvious the previous year's snowfall record would fall. I gave notice at *The Citizen.*

The idea of driving to Vancouver by Route 66 through the American southwest – the long way around – was to avoid the slightest possibility of snow. I did. It was 34°C in Albuquerque.

The day in February 1972 when I drove into Vancouver was overcast. It then proceeded to rain for 38 days and 39 nights – a not-quite-biblical experience. Within days I had migrated uphill. Like Noah on Mount Ararat, I found myself stranded high on a mountain – Grouse – above the end of Lonsdale Avenue. Higher than the rain clouds. A newcomer like me would not know that the higher you go in Vancouver, the wetter it gets.

In mid-July a Pacific cyclone dropped 45 mm of rain on the airport in 24 hours. At Hollyburn Ridge, which was more germane to my situation, 261 mm fell over 48 hours, causing flash-floods, filling basements all over the North Shore, and washing out bridges.

A rainstorm that Christmas Day broke the all-time 24-hour Vancouver precipitation record of 89.4 mm. It was worse where I lived.

But I stuck around. By then I was thoroughly acclimatized. Even this was an improvement over Ottawa.

– Sean Rossiter

Things looked pretty grim for the first month of Expo 86 . . . Colin Price, The Province

. . . but they picked up considerably. Starting July 17, Vancouver had its sunniest summer in 35 years, which helped draw crowds. Colin Price, The Province

seven weeks; it was the longest period without rain in 35 years in Vancouver. The first moisture in 53 days appeared on the 9th, but, at a piddling 0.2 mm, it was a sneeze from the weather gods. The last 13 days of Expo were rainless. Hundreds of thousands of people left Expo thinking they had been in Palm Springs without the palms.

Even with the splendid reputation its mild climate has given it, Vancouver still suffers from a bad rap. Allan Fotheringham once called Vancouver the Canadian city with the best climate and the worst weather. Vancouver may not have the best weather in British Columbia – Victoria does – but Vancouver's weather is better than most people give it credit for.

Vancouver is, for example, not Canada's wettest major city. Nor is it the second-wettest. Not even the third. In fact, no fewer than five cities in Canada have an average annual precipitation higher (or deeper) than Vancouver's paltry 1113 mm. Every city from Quebec City eastward to St. John's gets more annual precipitation than Vancouver. And, in

THE BRAKES!! NO?! NOT THE BRAKES?! AAAAAAGH!! STEER INTO THE SKID?? WHY DIDN'T I PUT MY SNOW TIRES ON?? AAAAAAGH!! Vancouver drivers deal with snow in their own special way. Rob Draper, The Vancouver Sun

Quebec City especially, you do have to shovel a lot of it.

In fact, the Climate Severity Index invented by Environment Canada confirms what anyone who had the sense to move to Vancouver or stay here already knew. Vancouver doesn't have the best weather in Canada, thank goodness. Vancouver comes second on the index. Just don't tell anybody. It's our little secret.

Okay?

Snow Shovel Memoirs

Fact: The winter of 1968-69 was snowier and colder in Vancouver than in Toronto. Observation: Because we do not believe in snow – in Vancouver, anyway – when snow does arrive, Vancouver 1) panics, or 2) tries to ignore it.

If you grew up in Ontario's snowbelt or the frigid prairies, you might think the average Vancouver driver would simply adjust by steering in the direction of the skid, or avoid using the brakes. At least clean off the back window.

But no. The whole idea of living in Vancouver is to have left behind the survival tactics the rest of the country lives by. We don't *want* to own galoshes; we wear sneakers in the snow, thank you very much. In Vancouver you have a less than one-in-ten chance of a White Christmas. This is a negligible price to pay.

When it snows, either you leave your car at home and swap snow-shovel memoirs with the other standees on the bus; or you drive normally, accelerating at yellow lights, signalling left-hand turns only after arriving within the intersection, and taking a good, fast run at uphill stretches, stopping for nothing. The result is fresh videotape on "The National" of the hillside Demolition Derby, set to an imaginatively ironic soundtrack – say, the Blue Danube Waltz.

The Toronto anchorman's patronizing tone and unheard chuckles from Corner Brook to Terrace are not the slightest bit embarrassing to that individual *Vancouver Sun* columnist Denny Boyd calls The Real Vancouverite:

Of course we can't drive in the snow! Who *wants* to be able to drive in the snow? *Why do you think we live here*?

Vancouver's Worst Winter Storm

A day like the one Vancouver had on January 21, 1935, would have been fairly normal in Edmonton. It might not even be news there. It would certainly be no excuse for arriving late at work.

In Vancouver, though, that day's 24-hour snowfall of 43 cm, whipped by gale-force winds and accompanied by -26°C temperatures, pretty much brought life to a frozen, messy standstill. It dominated the front pages. It was an all-time record snowfall for Vancouver.

But there was one added hazard that Edmonton would not have had to face: rain on the heels of a blizzard. Freezing rain forms ice on power lines and makes roads into hilly ice rinks. The sudden dip and rise in temperature, on top of the constant moisture of a Pacific Coast winter, is what makes a Vancouver storm dangerous.

The same system becomes deadlier as it moves east. If it persists into the snowfields of the Rockies, the result can be a heavy, frozen crust set on the frosty equivalent of ball bearings: snow melted and frozen again. By January 25, the storm had killed 11 people, many of them railroad workers, in avalanches from Sumas Mountain in the Fraser Valley to the Rogers Pass area.

In Vancouver in a serious snowstorm, the results are generally funny rather than sad: a cartoon strip with streetcars ambushed by snowdrifts, executives trapped in their offices – or retreating back to them and drying their socks on the radiators. Situation comedy material. "Orphans of Storm/Bare Feet and Steaming Socks in Offices/Marooned All Night," is how one *Sun* headline January 21 put it. Those who made it to work on time "had to plough through the snow that was more than two feet deep [60 cm] in drifts." *More than two feet deep!* The worst aftermath within Vancouver was the caved-in roof of the PNE Forum, the city's main hockey and curling rink.

We forget how easily Vancouver could be isolated in the days before all-weather air travel. Power lines were down from generators at Buntzen Lake and Stave Falls, Vancouver's main

In Chilliwack and throughout the Fraser Valley, power lines snapped under the weight of ice that accumulated in the winter storms of January 1935. Photo HP 50564, British Columbia Archives

sources of power. B.C. Electric appealed to the public to conserve light and heat. Electric range users were asked to do their evening cooking after 6 PM. A single telephone line connected B.C. with the outside world; that one led to Seattle.

As the rains continued to add to a snowmelt that had reached 120 cm, the Fraser Valley began to flood. Water to a depth of 5.8 m covered pasturelands as tributaries of the Lower Fraser overran their banks and undermined the Fraser dikes. Some farmers were forced to shoot their cattle.

As the rain turned to snow in the Interior and mountain uplands, effects that had been merely inconvenient turned deadly. Slowly, a death toll that has never been accurately determined began to be reported. Eleven avalanches crossed the railway line in four days near Rogers Pass alone, and six of the men working to clear the way were swept to their deaths. Train passengers in Calgary were delayed for a week as avalanches blocked the Rocky Mountain passes. Trappers were marooned in their cabins or the cabins themselves were swept away.

As people were being killed in the Interior of B.C. and the death toll climbed to nearly a dozen, a headline in the January 25th *Sun* showed how difficult it was for the papers to generate serious news in the city:

Havoc Among City Homes
Streets and Basements Under Water
Gardens Desolated

But the item that showed the true spirit of Vancouver under stress was this one:

"A man on Thirtieth Avenue is getting about in a canoe," *The Sun* reported on Page One that day "which, though leaky, he claims saves him the price of a pair of gumboots."

Another, perhaps more important indication was the fact that the BBC in London had seen fit to mention what was the worst storm in Vancouver's history. Until 1962, that is, when remnants of Typhoon Freda hit.

A HISTORY OF B.C. WEATHER WATCHING

It is nothing new for British Columbians to have their lives ruled by weather. Most coastal bands of natives had winter and summer homesites. Nootkan bands of mid-Vancouver Island spent their winters inland, near Tahsis, but camped out each summer at Yuquot, Nootka for "where the four winds blow." This exposed promontory at windy Nootka Sound was visited by Captain Cook in 1778 and was named Friendly Cove by James Strange when he arrived in 1786. The Englishmen might not have found the place so friendly had they arrived in winter.

A Stevenson Screen with louvres that protect the thermometer from direct sunlight. This is the basic weather data collection device for B.C.'s 550 weather observation stations. Environment Canada

First Stations and Forecasts

One thing about the English: when they colonized, they did a thorough job by first sending in the amateur weathermen of the Corps of Royal Engineers. Not only did the engineers survey the townsite of B.C.'s first capital, New Westminster, but they started recording weather there after 1859. New Westminster became an official meteorological station in 1874.

Although Victoria was a more important city, weather records were kept there only after 1880, and then by the Hudson's Bay Company. Meanwhile, the Engineers were operating the first Interior weather station at Spences Bridge on the Thompson River. During the 1870s Barkerville, centre of the Cariboo gold rush, became the biggest settlement west of Chicago and north of San Francisco. Logically enough, the main weather office for the Cariboo was set up at Barkerville – but not until 1888, when it was well on its way to becoming a ghost town. Kamloops, a strategic fur post in the late 1870s, and gateway to the gold fields, also had a recording station.

The Campbell-Stokes Recorder looks like a crystal ball, but it measures today's sunshine, not future weather. The glass sphere focuses the sun's rays on a card, leaving a burned trail whenever the sun shines. Environment Canada

Strong Winds (near 20 knots). Environment Canada

Strong Winds (near 30 knots). Environment Canada

Hazardous Winds

Term/Speed	*Sea States*
Strong winds 20-34 knots	Waves 3-6 m, white foam from breaking waves is blown along direction of wind. Small craft warning.
Gale 35-47 knots	Waves 6-9 m, crests begin to roll and tumble.
Storm 48-63 knots	Waves 9-16 m, very high waves with long overhanging crests. Surface of sea appears white.
Hurricane 64 or more	Waves more than 16 m filled with foam; sea completely white.

There were twenty such stations in B.C. by the mid-1880s, mainly along gold rush trails. These sudden mass migrations created the demand for weathermen to take the next, tricky step. It was all very well to record the weather. It would be quite another thing to forecast it.

With gold rushes breaking out every few years, Victoria businessmen who were outfitting prospectors wanted to be warned about Pacific storms that might delay shipments from San Francisco and the Orient. The Victoria merchants petitioned for forecasts, so it was no accident that the first government weather station in B.C. was built just outside Victoria in 1890.

But it took the better part of eight years for forecasts to be made available. The government estimated that forecasts would cost an additional $5000! B.C.'s first forecaster was E. Baynes Reed, superintendent of the Esquimalt station, and his first forecast appeared in *The Victoria Times* on November 1, 1898:

"These reports should prove of very great value to everyone," *The Times* asserted with evident pride, "and may be accepted with complete confidence by the public. The local office is in constant communication with San Francisco, Portland, Winnipeg and other points south and east, and is able to supply early warning of all variations in the weather . . ."

This first forecast read: "strong southwesterly winds, partly cloudy weather, with occa-

Gale Force Winds (near 40 knots). Environment Canada

Storm Force Winds (near 50 knots). Environment Canada

sional showers." The Lower Mainland would be "mostly cloudy, with showers."

That same year weather records began to be kept in Vancouver. More weather offices were established in the Interior, often by the Royal Engineers. Today about 550 weather recording stations are operated in B.C., mostly by volunteers.

Specialized Forecasts

Otherwise, the history of weather forecasting in B.C. is the story of industries that developed around the province during the first few decades of this century. Fruit growing was established in the mild climate of the Okanagan by 1935, when a frost warning unit was started there to save orchardists from sitting out all night, ready to light their smudge pots through the critical spring season.

British Columbia began to be important as Canada's doorway to the Pacific from the time of the clipper ships and tea trade, but with the coming of the airplane and war it became strategic. Weather forecasting became much more specific, detailing such information as the heights and extent of disturbances, visibility and wind speeds. Weather offices were opened at major airports. During the 1930s, when few aircraft could climb above the weather (almost all of which occurs below 6000 m), the accuracy of enroute forecasts became a matter of life and death – especially along mountain flightpaths.

With the coming of war in the Pacific, public weather forecasts were suspended. At a time when pillboxes were being built at Point Grey to send shivers through the Imperial Japanese fleet, it was felt that weather forecasts might aid enemy invasion plans.

For the armed forces, however, weather forecasts took on a new dimension. Prince George became a transit centre for the military buildup in Alaska. The main weather office for the Cariboo, moved to Prince George from Barkerville in 1929, became a northern forecast office for the U.S. Army Air Force.

With the phenomenal developments in airplane design during World War II came a demand for more sophisticated aviation forecasting. Prince George and Port Hardy became upper air data stations for gathering information for new pressurized bombers and transports that operated above 9000 m.

It was a small step from using weather forecasts in the war effort to using the same information in B.C.'s fight against forest fires. During the early 1950s a fire weather service was added to the regular public forecast. While the fire hazard is high, timber companies or the forest service often enforce closures or restrict cutting to predawn hours.

Since then other specialized forecasts have been made available to skiers, boaters, travellers through the mountains and highways personnel in winter, and to farmers during growing season. Marine forecasts are issued five times a day and aviation outlooks four times a day.

New Technology

These forecasts are the final products of a system that came into operation during the early sixties: a three-level process of refining forecasts from The Big Global Picture right down to Our Scenic Slocan Valley. It starts from nationwide maps drawn from a synopsis of trends around the globe and transmitted to regional centres, where they are further tailored to the needs of the region. Finally, meteorologists at local weather offices use their intimate knowledge of nearby valleys, lakes and mountains to produce the forecasts we hear and read every day.

Because most of B.C.'s weather systems originate over the Pacific and move east, weatherships were for many years the only way to monitor their progress to the coast. The first of these was stationed in the north Pacific during the war and was replaced by three converted navy frigates after 1950. They patrolled an area at 50° North latitude – roughly the border latitude – and 145° West longitude – which passes just east of Hawaii. During the 1960s, radar-equipped weatherships, the *Quadra* and the *Vancouver*, took over the station.

By 1979, the accelerating pace of weather technology had made even these purpose-built ships obsolete, and they were beached. By then, satellites were giving meteorologists views of any area in the world, each from a slightly-different angle. These satellites give ground-level temperatures, a temperature profile through the atmosphere, surface wind measurements and wave heights.

On the ground, Meteorological Automatic Reporting Stations (or MARS) record and transmit data. A new sea-level program from Environment Canada packs weather gear into shipping containers and pays the owners of freighters to carry them on deck. A reliable source of data is the balloons released from the fleets of automobile carriers bringing cars and trucks by the thousands east from Japan and South Korea.

Three weather buoys were anchored in a north-south line 300 km off the coast of Vancouver Island in 1987 as a kind of weather Distant Early Warning Line. They report hourly via satellite on winds, air temperature, moisture, sea state and atmospheric pressure. Boat-shaped, built at Sidney, B.C. at a cost of $300,000 each, they are anchored at a depth of 3600 m. Six smaller inshore buoys provide a secondary reporting line.

Environment Canada's Vancouver weather office was by then operational with a $150,000 radar system designed to provide site-specific forecasts of approaching storms during Expo 86. How well did it work? Perfectly, if you view carrying tools in your car trunk as a guarantee against roadside breakdowns: Vancouver had its second-longest period of rain-free weather during Expo.

Despite all these cosmic bells and whistles, it is still one thing to record the weather – every 30 minutes, right down to the wavetops – and something else entirely to predict what it will do three days from now.

Once a system passes the Maginot Line of buoys and radar, it can still go awry. As Gary Wells of Environment Canada's Pacific Region points out, when the storm hits the Vancouver Island mountains, the fronts are torn apart. A storm that exhibits uniform characteristics on its journey east can fall apart when it hits that wall of mountains. In 1962 remnants of Typhoon Freda hit Victoria, hit Vancouver, split, and doubled back to hit Victoria again. Who could have predicted that?

Environment Canada's climatologist in Vancouver, Earl Coatta, likes to emphasize

GOES goes. A Delta 179, carrying the GOES-H (Geostationary Operations Environmental Satellite) weather satellite, heads into the sky from Cape Canaveral. It transmits cloud images over North America from a geosynchronous, or stationary, orbit. NASA

NASA
DELTA
NOAA
179

This looks like a ship, but it's a weather buoy now anchored off Vancouver Island and providing hourly reports via satellite on air and sea conditions. Environment Canada

Weather balloons gather data from the upper atmosphere. Environment Canada

What Do They Mean by "Probability of Precipitation"?

0%	No precipitation even though it may be cloudy.
10%	Dry weather with only one chance in ten of snow or rain.
20%	Dry weather still expected.
30%	Go ahead with your picnic but you may have to take shelter.
40%	Umbrella recommended. Make other plans compatible with rain. Not a good day to paint the garage. Keep your fingers crossed.
50%	Even-stephen whether it rains or not. Be prepared.
60%	Lawn needs watering? Odds are Mother Nature might help.
70%	Maybe you should postpone outdoor events. Chances of dry weather: three in ten.
80%	Wet weather likely.
90%	Precipitation a near certainty. Venture out if you like walking in the rain.
100%	Rain or snow is a certainty.

that the weather forecast becomes more art than science the further it reaches into the future. Weather, especially over the north Pacific Ocean, has a mind of its own.

"We can track a storm for days," he says. "It moves due east, at a constant speed. We can predict when it will hit the coast of Vancouver Island. We have some idea of what will happen over the island on its way to the Lower Mainland. We know when it should arrive in Vancouver.

". . . And," says Coatta, "for whatever reason, it splits off on its own, suddenly turns right, and, in the case of cold lows of spring and early summer, meanders around and makes figure-eights."

How Accurate Are Environment Canada's Forecasts?

Eighty percent accurate, according to the 1988 *Weather Trivia Calendar*.

Who publishes the *Weather Trivia Calendar*?

The Canadian Government Publishing Centre, on behalf of Environment Canada.

There are, of course, many reasons Vancouver's weather is difficult to predict, despite the many technological advances made by the Weather Office during the 1980s.

The Lower Mainland consists of several microclimates at many altitudes. The question becomes: Vancouver's weather, but where? Hollyburn Ridge? Richmond? Or in the wind tunnel at Burrard and West Georgia?

Another reason, even with satellites, instrumented offshore buoys, and radar working every hour 24 hours a day, is a simple lack of data. Weather balloons are still an important source of atmospheric information, and for obvious reasons it is more difficult to release them over water than over land.

One big X-factor in weather on the Lower Mainland is that the topography makes it a *convergence zone*. Winds from many directions often converge over the open end of the Fraser Valley, sometimes creating thunderstorms on the spot.

Winds from Puget Sound heading north meet winds from the Strait of Juan de Fuca heading inland, mixing south of Vancouver over the San Juan Islands and heading north together, bringing with them – guess what?

An Environment Canada satellite photo of the Pineapple Express, the tropical front that caused millions of dollars of damage from flooding and rockslides in southwestern B.C. in November of 1990. While Kamloops had temperatures of 17°C, an arctic front from the north gave Williams Lake temperatures of -7°C and heavy snow. Environment Canada

Four main cloud types

Cirrus. Wispy cirrus clouds appear high in the sky and often signify an approaching storm. They can change to layered cirrostratus or cirrocumulus as the storm nears. Environment Canada

Stratus. Stratus clouds are low and uniform and can produce drizzle. At their lowest they are fog. Higher stratus clouds (altostratus and cirrostratus) don't produce precipitation. Environment Canada

Cumulus. Cumulus clouds have a flat base, like stratus, but build upwards. Puffy fairweather cumulus can produce showers when they develop into tall towers. If the billowing form occurs in layered clouds it is called stratocumulus (low), altocumulus (mid levels), or cirrocumulus (high levels). Environment Canada

Nimbus. Nimbus means rain. It occurs in two forms: nimbostratus, which is layered to great heights ahead of a front and produces steady rain, and cumulonimbus which has grown upward from a smaller cumulus cloud and produces heavy rain, thunder, lightning and sometimes hail. Environment Canada

B.C. WEATHER DISASTERS

Most often weather disasters in this part of the world are the outcome of days, weeks, even months of slowly building climatic effects. Thrill-seeking skiers who arrive by helicopter on virgin slopes late in a winter characterized by thawing and freezing bet their lives against an avalanche. Ninety-nine times out of a hundred they are right. When human folly meets extreme weather, results have often been catastrophic. These are stories about that hundredth time.

Rogers Pass Avalanche, 1910

At 5:40, about dusk on Friday, March 4, 1910, a small snowslide buried the Canadian Pacific Railway tracks in a narrow valley about a kilometre south of Rogers Pass, opposite snowshed #17. Sixty-two men – two section crews and a locomotive-driven rotary snow plow and its crew – were dispatched to the scene.

Despite the obvious hazards of the rugged terrain in the Selkirk Range of the Rocky Mountains, the next morning's *Province* reported, "the existence of snowsheds and a per-

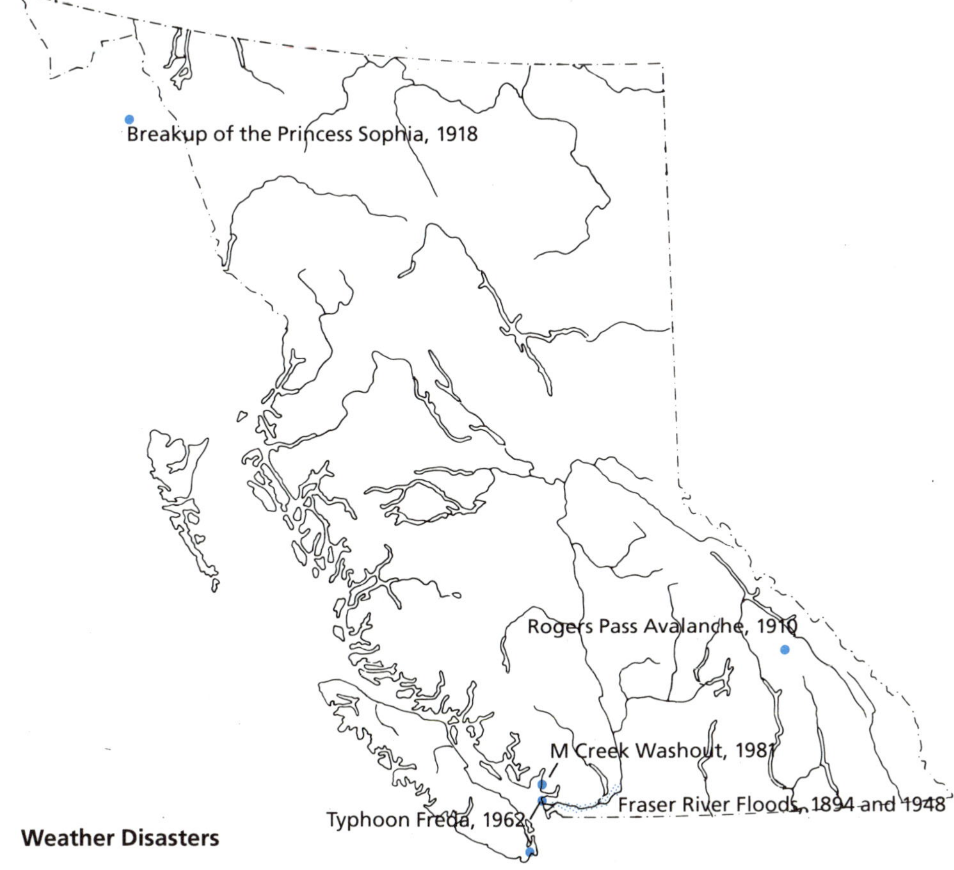

This base map has been reprinted with permission of the publisher from A.L. Farley, Atlas of British Columbia: People, Environment, and Resource Use *(Vancouver: UBC Press 1979). Copyright University of British Columbia Press. All rights reserved.*

fect system of patrolling the tracks near unprotected spots had hitherto, with rare exceptions, prevented any serious accident. No passenger or freight trains were ever swept away and no passenger ever lost his life . . ."

However, this enviable passenger safety record had cost the lives of more than 200 workers. Most of them had died in slides. No sooner had the National Dream been completed than it had to be abandoned to the elements for the winter. The next year, in 1887, construction began on 31 snowsheds to protect the railroad from the worst known slide areas around Rogers Pass: a total of 6.5 km of the rail line was roofed over. Each major accident or disaster led to improvements that made it safer.

CPR's Number 97 westbound express, bound for Vancouver with 400 passengers, was on its way into the Rocky Mountain foothills just as the slide at snowshed #17 was reported. Number 97 was known for having been struck by train robbers twice – once by the legendary Bill Miner.

Sleet was falling when the men and their equipment arrived. Sleet is characteristic of early-spring precipitation in the Selkirks. It

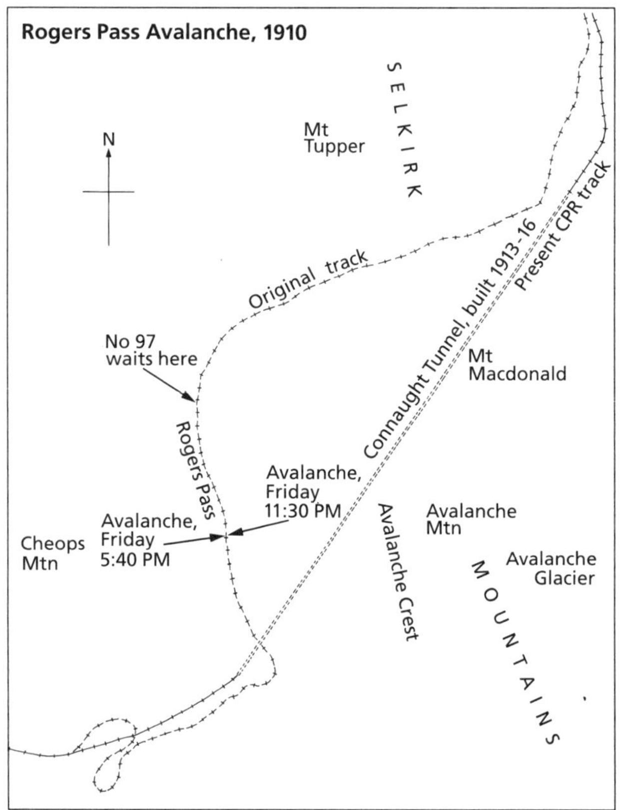

formed ice as night set in and the temperature fell, adding to the load on the surface of the snowpack. Alternating freezes and thaws create layers of hard and soft material in snowpacks. Farther down in the snow, drops of moisture freeze to the consistency of ball-bearings. As the weight of the top layers builds, the likelihood of avalanches increases. The winter of 1909-10 produced perfect conditions for avalanches. There had been many slides in late January and throughout February.

All around the section crew working at snowshed #17, the crack and boom of avalanches echoed from the surrounding peaks, some of them more than 3000 m high.

". . . The men, inured to such risks, stuck steadily to the task," according to *The Province's* account. "As the hours advanced the rain and sleet continued to fall in increasing volume."

Just before 11:30 PM Friday the tracks were almost clear. Only handwork was left to clean off the rails. The fireman on the rotary plow, Billy Lachance, climbed down from his engine and took a walk across the bridge over the creek far below. Soon after he arrived on the north bank, a sudden wind blasted up the mountainside – the first warning of an avalanche. The blast picked him up and threw him into some brush further up the slope. Then came the avalanche.

"In a few seconds, with a noise like a thousand thunderbolts crashing in unison, it leaped from shelf to shelf, uprooting and carrying with it a tangled mass of trees, ice, and huge boulders," the newspaper story related.

The snowpack near the cornice of Avalanche Crest, the ridge on the railroad's side of the canyon, gave way. The triangular slide, widening as it descended, engulfed 400 m of track, continued down into the chasm, plugging the stream, and roared up the north side, stopping virtually at Billy Lachance's feet.

The 91-tonne rotary plow and its locomotive were lifted and hurled upward 15 metres to the roof of a snowshed, where it was deposited upside-down. The wooden tender cars were reduced to matchwood and most of the crew were found buried underneath.

The next day 600 men, many of them log-

Rescuers survey the damage at the 1910 Rogers Pass avalanche. Photo HP59127 British Columbia Archives

gers and miners drafted from nearby camps, some brought from as far away as Calgary, were at work digging for the victims.

"I shall never forget the scene as I went down from our train to see them digging out the bodies of the unfortunate men," said Mr. C.G. Anderson, a salesman from Toronto who was aboard Number 97, stopped at Rogers Pass to await clear tracks.

"I saw the bodies of three white men and several Japanese taken out cold and stiff in death. Every one of these men were (sic) found in an upright position . . . The hands of nearly all the victims were extended in front of their faces as though they had been animated with the idea of self-preservation in the fatal moment when the avalanche descended."

Two of the Japanese men were buried in each other's embrace. Two foremen were buried facing each other, as if chatting. Another man was found with a cigarette paper in his hand, caught rolling a smoke. Big, powerful D.J. McDonald, the area's bridge foreman,

The wreckage of the locomotive and its rotary plow in the 1910 avalanche at Rogers Pass. Photo HP59129 British Columbia Archives

Weapons in the war against snow. A 105 mm howitzer takes aim at an unstable slide path to create a controlled avalanche. Better forecasting and prevention techniques are limiting disastrous avalanches. John G. Woods, Canadian Parks Service

had begun to struggle out from under almost two metres of snow, but died half way. All were suffocated.

Over the next two years nearly 100 slides occurred in Rogers Pass. In 1913 the CPR broke down and authorized the drilling of the 8-km Connaught Tunnel straight through the granite core of the mountain to avoid the pass altogether, a project that took three years and $9.2 million ($2.5 million for dynamite) to complete.

Rogers Pass no longer exists as part of the CPR-VIA Rail mainline. Billy Lachance, released soon after from hospital in Revelstoke, never went back to the railroad.

Avalanche Hazards

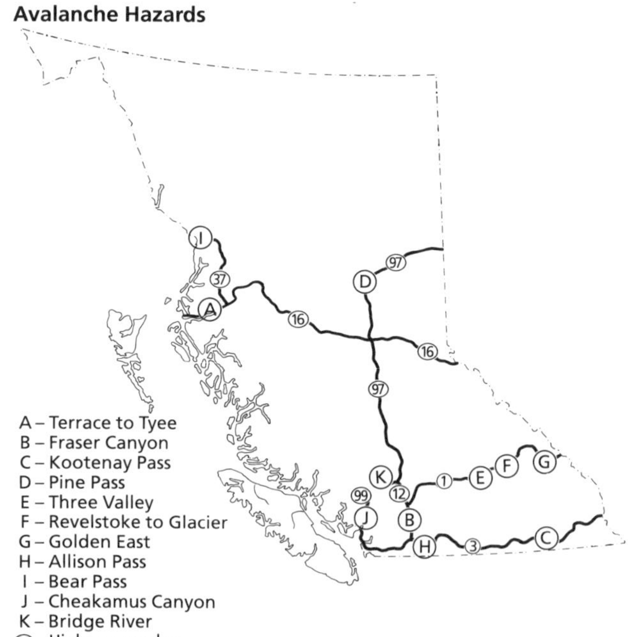

This base map has been reprinted with permission of the publisher from A.L. Farley, Atlas of British Columbia: People, Environment, and Resource Use (Vancouver: UBC Press 1979). Copyright University of British Columbia Press. All rights reserved.

Breakup of the Princess Sophia, 1918

Captain Leonard P. Locke was within a few months of retirement, and his last command, the CPR steamer *Princess Sophia,* was overloaded when she left Skagway. Captain Locke, a Haligonian who had gone to sea at 16, served much of his career on the Liverpool-New York run and joined the CPR fleet in 1891. He was no stranger to heavy weather and high seas. "... Everybody says that Captain Locke knows every inch up to Skagway," one of the ship's firemen wrote home to his wife, "so we are safe as far as that goes."

So when the blizzard struck, driven by 80-km/h winds out of the northeast that whipped the icy waters of the Panhandle into 8-metre waves, Locke and his pilot maintained full speed ahead: 11 or 12 knots. Visibility was perhaps 100 metres. Locke was accustomed to using the ship's whistle as a primitive form of radar by listening for echoes off the cliffs to either side, but this time the wind may have interfered with the return signal. Five hours out of Skagway at 3 AM Thursday, October 24, the *Sophia* hit Vanderbilt Reef. The ship ran fully two-thirds of her length onto the rock.

After the initial shock, there was no panic. The ship's boats were made ready and a few partly lowered, but not launched. Most of the passengers returned to their berths. At the 6 AM high tide, with the seas still pounding, the *Sophia*'s stern began to float off the reef. But the starboard bow ground and slipped on the rock, settling into a groove.

The bow remained fast, but the stern was pounded by the gale-force storm blowing from directly behind. Vanderbilt Reef, the peak of a thousand-foot underwater mountain, is only 64 km from Juneau, where the narrow north-south Lynn Canal opens to the sea. The mountains to the west of Lynn Canal usually protect it from Pacific storms, but when the wind blows out of the north, as it did then, the arctic blast is intensified by the sheer cliffs to either side.

A well-built six-year-old steamer, the *Princess Sophia* was a product of the Paisley shipyard in Scotland, then the foremost shipbuilding nation in the world. Comfortably appointed – "palatial, yacht-like," as the CPR advertised it – and structurally sound, it had a double steel bottom. Its outer hull was badly damaged by the impact with the reef and its main steam pipe broken, but the ship took on water only at the bow. Locke seemed unperturbed.

At least three ships had been wrecked on Vanderbilt Reef, but Locke was probably also aware that eight years before, another CPR boat had run onto the same rock, been pulled off, and returned to service.

Eight American boats appeared that day, including the lighthouse tender U.S.S. *Cedar,* which was big enough to take all of the *Sophia*'s crew and passengers. But the *Cedar* and its accompanying fleet of tugs and fishboats had to retreat overnight behind nearby islands for refuge from the storm.

The next day, Friday, only got worse. The barometer began to fall; some estimates of the wind speed put it at 130 km/h. Most of what we know about the disaster comes from accounts written that day in letters and wills found on the victims. Twice that morning Captain John Leadbetter anchored the *Cedar* downwind of the *Sophia* but the force of the wind and waves dragged the anchor along the inlet floor. Everyone on the scene agreed that the passengers aboard the *Sophia* were safer where they were. As the weather deteriorated, the smaller boats were forced back to their island retreat.

At 4:50 that afternoon, this message was received by the *Cedar* through the snowy gloom:

"Taking water and foundering. For God's sake come and save us."

The *Cedar* replied:

"Coming full speed, but cannot see on account of thick snow and heavy seas."

Subsequent messages from the Sophia became weaker until the *Cedar* suggested saving the radio for the worst.

Now the wind and waves began to turn the Sophia 180 degrees, grinding her plates so the top of the reef was polished smooth, dropping the stern into the frigid waters, and the ship

Riding high – Princess Sophia stuck on Vanderbilt Reef, lifeboats swung out but not launched. It didn't seem to be an emergency until a storm made rescue impossible. Except for a dog, all aboard were lost. Photo HP78026 British Columbia Archives

slid backward into the towering waves. The boiler room flooded and the boilers exploded. Portholes were shattered and part of the deck blown off. Most of the *Sophia*'s supply of bunker oil for a voyage barely begun now was released to the sea, where it congealed. No general alert had been ordered. It all happened too fast.

At 5:20 came her final message:

"For God's sake hurry. Water coming in the room." Wireless operator David Robinson begged the *Cedar*'s radio man to keep talking to him for reassurance.

After half an hour the *Cedar* was forced to abandon its rescue. The snow was blowing horizontally, making it impossible for Capt. Leadbetter to see his own ship's bow.

All the *Cedar* found at first light Saturday was the *Sophia*'s foremast. Even the oil slick was gone. The bodies began to wash up on nearby shores later Saturday and Sunday. Four women were found lashed to an inflatable raft, evidence to *The Vancouver Daily Sun* that "Britain's traditions in disasters at sea – beginning with the cry 'Women first' – were in the minds of the *Sophia*'s crew when they realized that they faced death in the raging waters." Almost all of the 353 victims were found not to have drowned but suffocated in the oil slick.

The worst marine disaster on the Pacific coast was headline news the following week in Vancouver and Victoria as the *Princess Alice* delivered its cargo of coffins to each city. The sole survivor of the *Princess Sophia* was an oil-soaked English setter that must have swum 13 km and struggled a further six to the hamlet of Auk Bay.

Fraser River Floods, 1894 and 1948

No single feature of British Columbia reflects its seasonal weather moods as closely as the Fraser River. Its pulse ebbs and flows over a fantastic scale: the average March flow of 71,000 cubic metres normally increases more than tenfold by June, to 850,000 – or more. The snowpack from a hard winter along the Alberta border, melted by above-normal temperatures in April and May, can cause the river to re-occupy much of its valley and delta, flooding the best farmland in B.C. and cutting off our most populous region from the rest of the country.

The 1894 Flood

A long, hard winter in 1893-94 filled the Rocky Mountain watershed with snow, and the Fraser began to rise in May, as usual. Toward the end of the month, though, bad news began to filter in from the Interior. On May 29 it was reported that above Yale bridges and fillings were washed out from the railroad bed. Trains were delayed. The next day dikes crumbled hours apart at Hatzic, Fort Langley and Matsqui, one after another. Thousands of hectares were flooded by each breach.

Still the waters rose. Lowlands throughout the entire Pacific Northwest were inundated. Portland, Oregon was also underwater. The suspension bridge at Spuzzum, an engineering marvel when it was built, was washed out. At Craigellachie, site of the CPR's Last Spike, the bridge and 150 metres of track were under 2 metres of water. A thousand men were at work there. Workmen spotted a raft floating downstream on the Fraser with a family of five, all dead and securely lashed onboard.

Annacis Island was under several feet of water. Three steamers were chartered by the provincial government to cruise the 160-by-24-km disaster area to rescue people from the upper stories of their homes and cattle from islands and high ground. Most docks were well

Row, row, row your boat gently down the street . . . the 1894 Fraser River flood at Chilliwack. Photo HP10337 British Columbia Archives

underwater. Boats tied up to those railway tracks that were still visible. At Chilliwack, churchgoers paddled to services in canoes, which they tied up to their pews. Brodie's cannery on Deas Island was simply washed away.

In early June, temperatures at various points in the Interior soared to 38°C. Only on June 10 did it become clear that the waters were receding.

Dikes were built at Maple Ridge, Matsqui, and near Chilliwack in the next two years. After the First World War an ambitious project to reclaim 12,000 hectares in the Sumas district was carried out at the then-incredible cost of $1.8 million. These investments seemed justified as the annual late-spring pulse of the Fraser River was contained within its normal banks.

BC's Pulse: the Fraser River

The Fraser River drains one-quarter of the province (with its tributaries, more like one-third), running 1368 km in a vast loop from the western slopes of the Rockies just south of 3954-metre Mount Robson (near Jasper), northwest through the Rocky Mountain Trench to Prince George. There it turns south down the Interior Plateau through a bedrock canyon its rushing waters have cut to a depth, in places, of 600 metres.

At Hope, the Fraser turns west to course through the valley it created and once fully covered, a valley that opens, at the river's delta on the Strait of Georgia, to 80 km in width. There, at the narrow head of the valley, the river is only five metres above sea level, depending on the season. It has been filling its channels over the past 50 million years with materials carried down from the Interior: a 1.5-km layer of silt built up on the valley floor. By the time it passes New Westminster, Bruce Hutchison observed 40 years ago, "the clear mountain water has become so heavy with the freight of the Clay Belt as to seem almost solid enough to walk on." The Fraser created the Lower Mainland with its deposits, providing the humpbacked gravel site of Vancouver and its suburbs, which house half the population of B.C.

The 1948 Flood

Seen in the light of the subsequent flood, it is all too tempting to see any development of the valley as folly. But the population of the valley had increased from 1,000 in 1894 to 50,000 by 1948. Industry was relocating there from Vancouver. It took a singular series of conditions to set the table for a flood that made 1894 look like a lifeboat drill.

Spring came late to most of B.C. in 1948. Unseasonably cold weather delayed the snowmelt. It was well into May before the runoff began. When it did, no previous measurement of the river's fury had any meaning. At Grand Forks on May 26 the Kettle River was 2.4 m over its banks, and, at Kimberley, Mark Creek was sweeping houses off their foundations. Tragedy was working its way down the tributaries of the mighty Fraser in a landlocked tidal wave coming south and west. Only a dramatic drop in temperatures over the snowpack could save the valley.

The river rose a full metre May 25, passing the danger point the next day. That day, the 26th, the dike at Agassiz gave way, and the Fraser was 1.6 km wide at that point. The worst flood in Canadian history was underway. At the same time that Agassiz found itself under a metre of water, fire broke out when the water reached a warehouse supply of lime. Eventually, the water rose 30 cm higher at the Mission gauge than the 1894 peak.

Within days of the full dimensions of the flood becoming clear, what was left of Canada's war machine was brought in to undertake its biggest peacetime manoeuvres ever. They called it Operation Overflow.

Where three chartered river boats steamed to the rescue in 1894, navy minesweepers and landing craft cruised the muddy currents in May and June 1948, searching for survivors. Volunteer powerboat operators fanned out from the frigate HMCS *Antigonish* off the New Westminster docks, recalling the civil fleet that rescued the British Army at Dunkirk.

Princess Patricia's Light Infantry, airlifted from Calgary, took up the infantryman's shovel to fill sandbags once again three years after

Soldiers returned home from World War II to find another battle on their hands, this time against Mother Nature and the 1948 Fraser River flood. Vancouver Sun

returning from Europe. They patrolled the dikes with flare pistols, searching for breaks.

The RCAF first flew tents out of Vancouver in war-surplus Canso flying-boats to house the homeless in Kimberley and Grand Forks, then turned around and brought soldiers, sandbags, and, finally, food, west with the flood tide.

At home in Vancouver, the papers were calling the valley "the 100-mile battlefront." Provincial, then national states of emergency were declared. President Harry Truman declared the U.S. Pacific Northwest a disaster area. Butter and meat were rationed in Vancouver. (Then again, fruits and vegetables bound for points east were held up and sold at discount prices. Fresh fish was "clogging the local market.")

As in any war, false dawns and momentary victories teased the foot soldiers. When the waters of the Fraser fell at Prince George on June 1, there was hope that the rush of water over the valley would soon slacken. But the next day the dike at Hatzic Lake gave way, the Fraser propelled two houses into the lake, and the army appealed for 700 more volunteers.

Now, with the railway and the Trans-Canada washed out, the Lower Mainland was

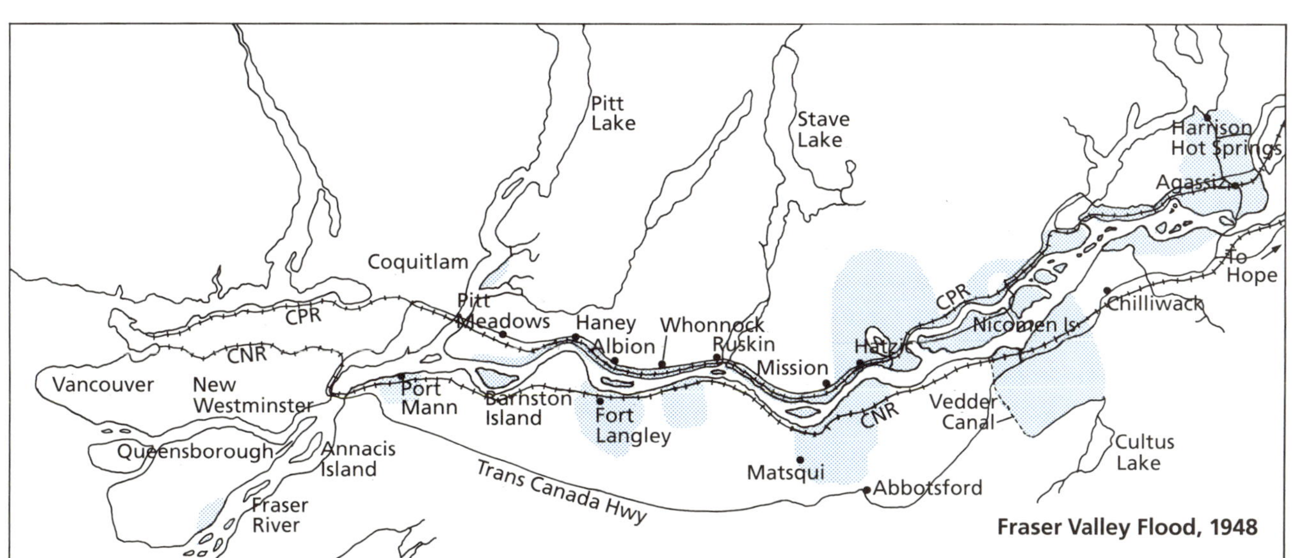

Fraser Valley Flood, 1948

isolated except by air. The raised and double-tracked CPR mainline, as a caption under a huge photo of the devastation explained, was "twisted into useless pretzels."

June 5 turned out to be the hottest day of the year. In from the Prairies came more soldiers – Lord Strathcona's Horse – to shore up the dikes at Lulu Island. The mayor of Blaine arrived with 100 more volunteers. Profiteers bought stranded cattle for $10 a head. The old Hotel Vancouver at Georgia and Granville, first written off in 1920 but used in World War II as officers' quarters, housed refugees.

The waters rose on June 10. Heavy rains fell, threatening to compound the disaster at its worst point. It was only then, at the darkest hour of 1948, that the flood took an unexpected turn for the better.

On the 11th the same bright sunshine that had hitherto been an ill omen became, for the first time, a friend soaking up some of the water. The floodwaters fell that day for the first time. As it so often has in the annals of war, victory came late and in disguise.

Typhoon Freda, 1962

The remnants of Typhoon Freda did the most lasting damage to Victoria and Vancouver of any storm. It struck hardest at Vancouver's soul: Stanley Park.

Freda began life as a lazy, meandering little typhoon, stumbling around the South Pacific a week before it arrived in B.C. There was little to be alarmed about. Regular bulletins were forwarded from Japan about this 8-km/h disturbance. Twenty-four hours later it was being referred to practically in the past tense. (Typhoons and hurricanes are the same: hurricanes occur along the eastern Pacific and the Atlantic seaboard; typhoons along the western Pacific.)

The next day it was gathering power and speed. By noon on the 10th it had passed the International Dateline in the mid-Pacific, had settled on an easterly course, veered south to threaten southern California, and then, on October 12, began a 62-km/h swing to the north, hitting the Oregon Coast and slowing – but still vicious enough to have areas of all three Pacific states declared disaster areas. Twenty-five people were killed along the U.S. west coast.

A fairly serious storm hit Vancouver on the Thursday before Freda hit. It caused power outages, a death from electrocution and much damage to small boats. That storm gathered strength as it moved north, becoming the worst storm in 20 years in Nanaimo, gusting to 104 km/h at Comox. But this storm had almost no warning value. Who would have guessed that a much more vicious storm was following so closely?

As Freda moved over the Olympic Peninsula, which normally shields Victoria from the worst effects of storms, it speeded up again. Moving at 74 km/h, it struck B.C.'s capital at 11 PM Friday. Within the storm were gusts of up to 145 km/h, fluctuating from gale force to hurricane force.

The gale caused the worst damage to power transmission systems in B.C. Hydro's history and severed all telegraph circuits and most long-distance phone lines from Victoria to the mainland. A large motor vessel, the *Chatham Chief II*, was beached, anchor and all, well above the normal tideline at Cadboro Bay. A 38-tonne example of the biggest flying-boat manufactured during the Second World War, a four-engine Martin Mars water-bomber, had its half-inch steel mooring cables snapped, its rudder and elevator surfaces ripped off, and was driven 187.5 metres across Patricia Bay Airport and wrecked.

The storm then made its way across the Strait of Georgia to Vancouver. Freda was not through with Victoria yet, however. It split after hitting Vancouver, half the storm doubling back to Victoria, and half charging up-coast toward Terrace.

This time Freda was heralded in Victoria by winds gusting to 131 km/h. It hit Vancouver moving faster as a whole than it had hit Victoria, but with gusts slightly diminished at 101 km/h – just short of the record wind velocity for Vancouver International Airport. This was, remember, only the remnants of a tropical storm.

Hydro pole transformers explode during Typhoon Freda. Eric Lindsay, Photo CVA 392-1083, City of Vancouver Archives

Vancouver felt its fury for no less than four hours, starting at 12:35 AM Saturday. Seven people were killed overnight: four in cars hit by toppled trees, one when his car was blown out of control, and two who succumbed to heart attacks after climbing to their roofs to repair TV aerials during the Late-Late Show. One-fifth of Stanley Park's treed acreage was blown down.

Suspended traffic lights were blown horizontal. Vancouver's tallest church spire, surmounting the Evangelistic Tabernacle, was wrenched from its roof and deposited in the sanctuary.

Half the area from Horseshoe Bay to Hope was without power. With electricity failing almost everywhere, "It kept getting darker and darker until it was pitch black," said Brian Kent, a *Sun* photographer assigned to record the devastation. "Then you could see these things that looked like snakes jumping over the ground. They were fallen electrical wires that moved every time they hit something metal." Kent found that he was unable to drive across Vancouver's bridges at the height of the storm in one of the Volkswagen Beetles supplied by the newspaper to its photographers.

Most of the damage was repairable. The lost evergreens in Stanley Park, the mature ones more than 60 years old, were replaced in nature's order of things by alder and maple, the first species to grow in open spaces in the forest. But Stanley Park is not a deciduous forest. Nearly 30 years later, the question of what to do with the natural intruder replacements resurfaced: they would be logged and replaced by conifer seedlings artificially hand-planted by MacMillan-Bloedel.

M Creek Washout, 1981

Driving alongside Howe Sound's brooding splendour can exact a price, as the numerous signs warning of Falling Rock, and indentations and cracks in the pavement remind us. Tom Willey, then 24 and a resident of Britannia Beach, came close to paying that penalty.

The night of October 27, 1981 was black and windy, and continued several days of torrential rains on the North Shore of Burrard Inlet and up Howe Sound. Tom Willey figures that sitting as high as he did in his pickup truck may have enabled him to see the abyss in front of him a split second sooner than the two drivers ahead of him. It was difficult enough to see the highway with the masses of autumn leaves that were being blown across it. Once Willey's front wheels hit the wet plank surface of the south end of the bridge, his brakes were worse than useless. Having the front wheels of his truck slide over the edge of the washed-out 18-metre centre span of the M Creek timber bridge may be what got it stopped. The pickup's frame took the impact.

Two vehicles, a car and a van with five passengers each, had already plunged into the ooze of mud carrying rocks, uprooted trees, and the remains of the bridge down the bloated creekbed 15 m below, to the Sound. "It was like lava flowing," recalls Murray Lund, the RCMP constable who was first on the scene.

No sooner had Willey got his truck stopped than the glare in his rear-view mirror told him another driver was bearing down on him.

"I thought he'd hit me for sure and I'd be a goner – right over the edge. But instead at the last moment he pulled out and went around me and right over the edge. They found his body two days later."

It was a miracle that anyone in the vehicles that fell survived. Joe Chisholm, the 21-year-old driver of the car that was on the bridge when it collapsed, remembered only that he had braked, and then felt his car falling. It landed on its wheels, but rolled down the gully to the Sound. Chisholm broke his nose and his three backseat passengers escaped through

The force of the M Creek torrent washed away two houses. The normally 1.2-metre creekbed became a 10-metre sluiceway of slime that carried 70 metres of railway into Howe Sound. Wayne Leidenfrost, The Province

The M Creek torrent took this Highway 99 bridge and three vehicles with it. The bridge's design was its downfall. Wayne Leidenfrost, The Province

the broken rear window, but the 17-year-old girl beside him in the front seat was killed.

All but one of the George family of the Axen Reserve near Squamish were killed in their van. Tom Willey and Don Gaulder of Squamish rescued four people from the gorge that night.

The M Creek bridge was a carefully maintained and well-built trestle-type timber structure, anchored at bedrock and amply cross-braced. Unfortunately, the profusion of struts, columns and trusses holding it up was its undoing: there were no open arches for the debris torrent to pass through. The bridge's replacement was already being designed at the time.

Its engineers could never have anticipated a flow of such volume as to turn the normally 1.2 metre-wide creek into a torrent that carried uncountable tonnes of debris and the bridge's centre span down its gorge, washing out 70 metres of railway line, carrying the house at its mouth into the Sound and undermining another. Afterward, the slimy mix extended 10 metres on either side of the normal creekbed.

Being set into to the windward side of a steep slope that rises out of a fjord, as Highway 99 is, exposes the road to the worst of coastal weather hazards. The water of the Sound only exaggerates the orographic effect of heavy rainfall on the west slopes of its eastern shore. Clouds form, rise, and lose their moisture quickly. Winds can come from almost any direction. An abnormally wet winter can prevent the formation of snowpack, thus spreading the runoff from such a winter over a longer period.

Geology of Howe Sound

As recently as 90,000 years ago, there were active volcanos in the Pacific Range of the Coast Mountains along Howe Sound. The newer volcanic rock is even less stable than the igneous quartz rock that pushed up millions of years ago from beneath the earth's crust and formed these mountains. Thanks to the 2-km-thick glacier that covered Vancouver and the peaks overlooking the Sound – and helped gouge out the fjord – masses of sedimentary rocks and loose debris, such as gravel, sit atop the range's unstable foundation. Much of that debris was deposited practically yesterday – 13,000 to 15,000 years ago, when the glacier was receding and sea level was up to 150 m higher that it is now. It sat at or above the level of the railroad and highway. From Lions Bay to Britannia, there are four sand and gravel quarries, some of them left from Ice Age streambeds. A drive up Howe Sound is a non-stop busman's holiday for geologists: the cliffs bear the scars of 174 million years of unimaginable turmoil.

The highway bridges 26 creeks along the twisting 40-km stretch from Horseshoe Bay to Britannia Beach, and half of these creeks have erupted in floods or debris torrents since 1906 – a total of 31 floods or torrents.

A flood consists mostly of water overflowing a creek's normal confines. A debris torrent can consist almost entirely of mud, carrying boulders, logs, and uprooted trees. Floods tend to undermine chunks of pavement on the highway, while a debris torrent, like the one that roared down the bed of M Creek the night of October 28, 1981, can take out a substantial bridge.

From 1906 to 1981, 49 persons lost their lives from debris torrents and floods on the slopes above eastern shore of Howe Sound. Thirty-seven of those deaths occurred in a nearly-forgotten flood of Britannia Creek in 1921. Exactly 60 years to the day before M Creek erupted, nearly half the houses in Britannia Beach were swept away or otherwise damaged by a 25-metre-high "wall of water" that descended along Britannia Creek.

The highway itself, known to the newspapers as the "Highway of Death," has accumulated its own accident toll. Its blind curves and hairpin turns require scrupulous attention even under the best conditions. The road has constantly been improved: it is wider and straighter in places, rock overhangs have been pared back, it has been underpinned with concrete-block walls along its outer margins, and, of course, new concrete bridges have replaced timber crossings. As more traffic is drawn up the Squamish Highway by increased development at Whistler-Blackcomb, and more subdivisions are built uphill from the road, the more elaborate and expensive the solutions will become.

"There's a lot of weather here."
– Grady Hall,
left-handed pitcher,
Vancouver Canadians

Not only is there a lot of weather in British Columbia, we spend a lot of time out in it. There are more kinds of weather in B.C. than anywhere else in the country, and, although it cannot be scientifically proven, we know that British Columbians do more out in the weather than other Canadians.

What the Pros Say

Just keeping track of the weather – let alone forecasting it accurately – is an immense undertaking, involving hundreds of people from backyard weather recorders to the staff of Environment Canada. But then the stakes most British Columbians have in the weather are high.

"I'm not sure people believe the forecast," says a radio-station program director. "In fact," he says, "there are studies that say most people don't – but they sure love to hear about the weather."

How do people react to the weather? As with any burning public issue, the person to ask is a cab driver.

"Rain is bad, but low clouds really bug people as well," says one of several drivers awaiting their shifts in Vancouver's Black Top Cabs ready room. "Especially if they stay low for a few days. No kidding: they find fault with everything – the taxi, the driver, the traffic, you name it."

Bad weather may be good news for cabbies – the worse the weather gets, the better – but if the rain drags on over a period of days, "you get people who don't always use a taxi so they don't know about tipping. Tips go way down."

"I only notice (bad moods) if it rains for a while," says a B.C. Transit bus driver. "Mostly they know it could be a lot worse somewhere else. At least this way the grass stays green."

The last individual you would expect to be guided by the weather is the butcher. But, as *The Vancouver Sun* reports, the namesake of Peter Black & Sons Butchers "charts his course like a sailor. Clouds don't bring rain for Black, they bring customers wanting stewing meat, oxtails and pot roasts. When the sun breaks out, so do the T-bones."

The police, of course, are also full-time students of human nature. Crime seems to rise under a full moon – a phenomenon that falls outside the scope of this book. But no constable needs to consult statistics to know that the police are busiest in July, when it is hot, and in February, in the depressing depths of a dank, dreary coastal winter. Only the victims differ. Crimes of violence peak during the long dog days; the violence is self-inflicted during the short days and long lonely nights of the suicide season.

Personal Climate Control

W.S. Kals, the footloose author of *Your Health, Your Moods, and The Weather,* had lived happily in Antwerp for several years but had decided to move to Canada. Where should he settle? His research "revealed a city called Vancouver as having temperatures closely resembling Antwerp . . . So that's where I went. I stayed 16 years and never regretted it."

Where does he live now? Florida.

SAD, Seasonal Affective Disorder, is thought to be caused by grey, low-light winters, just like the ones – uh-oh – on the coast. Wayne Leidenfrost, The Province

Reacting to Weather

Clinical studies are only beginning to probe the mystery of how weather affects us. Scientists are still at an early stage in understanding how high and low pressure systems affect people's lives. But we can make some early, tentative observations.

Demographers, who study populations and their movement, know that many people live in B.C. precisely *because* of the weather. That makes this province something of a laboratory for the study of weather effects on people. It is intriguing to learn, for example, that while the residents of other provinces are attracted by our mild coastal winters, those of us who live here are subject to unique forms of winter depression.

Those photos of sails bobbing on English Bay that appear in eastern newspapers just as snowdrifts reach the eaves in the rest of the country are one reason three in ten Canadians would, on the whole, rather live in B.C. It comes as no surprise that the province with the most people dying to get out is Manitoba, where 34 percent, or 350,000 people, would be happy to move. Half of those would prefer to live in B.C.

"Generally, Manitobans are very proud of their province," former premier Howard Pawley said in reaction to a nationwide survey in 1986, shortly before he lost his last election, "but there is a climatic factor that enters into it." Perhaps some of Pawley's supporters had moved further west.

We understand how they feel each time we travel to other parts of Canada in winter or early spring. Returning from a trip to, say, Calgary or Ottawa, luxuriating in the green grass and daffodils is as much of a life-affirming experience as anyone could ask for.

Most people are aware that they feel less excited during the short, dim days of winter – especially along the coast, where there are few bright, cloudless days from October to May. We sleep longer, eat more, stop exercising, crave carbohydrates and gain weight. Almost all of us feel these symptoms to a greater or lesser degree. They are universal enough to

Arthur Erickson's Gordon Smith House was designed in 1964 to maximize wintertime low light levels on the coast.
Arthur Erickson Architects

have become a topic of scientific study with a name, Seasonal Affective Disorder (SAD), and treatment techniques that are still evolving.

There are two theories about what causes SAD. One involves the shorter daylight period, which the body senses and adapts to. Some animals, for example, hibernate. The other theory suggests that the total amount of white light is sensed by the body, which responds to a decrease over each 24-hour period in winter. While most specialists seem to believe the decrease in the "photoperiod" during winter causes SAD, they are looking to white light as a possible therapy.

Patients are exposed to full-spectrum lights, five times as powerful as normal office lighting, for varying periods and at different times of the day. Bright light, it seems, inhibits the pineal gland's production of a hormone called meltonin, a depressant that induces sleep and regulates the reproductive cycles of animals.

Of course, there are other ways to combat SAD. For most of those who suffer from a Pacific coastal winter's dim, diffused light and short days, it is a simple question of which they can afford: bright-light therapy or a week on Maui.

The quality of its light may be one reason Vancouver has produced so many outstanding architects. Most of us think of architects as working with such materials as steel, bricks and concrete. But architects will tell you they work with light.

"Light gives life to architecture by changing its volumetric effects and subtle intimations of mood," Arthur Erickson has written. ". . . Light can be hard or glaring, or ineffably soft and luminous . . . The coast demands that buildings be transparent to light, by means of walls of glass or skylights that permit a gentle introspective light to bathe the walls, or water to reflect the sky's brightness from the earth's dark surfaces."

Victoria used to be "heaven's lobby," but now retirees of all ages are taking advantage of the Okanagan's dry climate. Province of British Columbia

Working in Weather

Good or bad, weather rules our lives. A string of hot, dry weeks during the summer is an increasingly common trend, welcome in the city and cause for worry outside it.

In the woods, of course, such a rain-free period can mean a red-zone forest-fire hazard, as it did in 1985. All of the Kootenays seemed to be ablaze that summer. The damage in lost timber and cost of fire fighting came to $300 million that year. Loggers lose their longest, most productive working days during such periods. Not to mention the threat to towns like Grand Forks.

Nowhere is the weather less predictable and more critical than in the north. Stewart is located along the Alaska Panhandle. Until very recently, Stewart's air link with Prince Rupert was by Grumman Goose, a World War II amphibian with the advantage of being able to alight on land or sea but no blind-flying equipment. If it was snowing, as it often was, the only way out of Stewart was by driving, often through white-out conditions, to Terrace. Terrace was connected by all-weather jet airliners with Vancouver. During the past few years, airline deregulation has brought more modern radar-equipped, turboprop aircraft which can operate from northern outposts with short gravel strips. But in many places you can still make all the plane reservations you want, but you don't know whether you will be going anywhere until takeoff.

If there is a time in most people's lives when they would just as soon eliminate guesswork about the weather, it is when they retire. For that reason, Victoria and the Gulf Islands, secure in the rain-shadow of Washington State's Olympic Mountains, have long been the most popular retirement destinations in Canada. But Kelowna offers an even more uniform climate that has led to its recently being called Palm Springs North.

The Globe and Mail has reported that Kelowna's population of 100,000 is rising by ten people a day, and it has been estimated that nearly 40 percent of home buyers there are more than 55 years old – even though the Chamber of Commerce says that senior citizens account for only 28 percent of the population.

Even as economic activity subsided in most of Canada during the early 1990s, Kelowna was booming. A new form of subdivision – "the walled city" – has been imported from California to cater to security-conscious seniors. Situated inside high walls with locked gates, townhouses have become more expensive in Kelowna than single-family detached houses. Some seniors' developments offer everything from condominiums to extended-care rooms. The city's development director notes that in 1990 Kelowna was processing more building permit applications than the provinces of Manitoba, Saskatchewan or New Brunswick.

More than most, the livelihoods of fruit-growers depend on weather. Any change from normal temperatures or rainfall, especially in early spring, can mean disaster for B.C.'s fruit growers, most of whom are located, like Kelowna, in the Okanagan Valley.

Its desert-like climate, the reason so many people retire there, is what makes the Okanagan such a great place to grow peaches, apricots, apples and cherries. The weather is predictable and the changes of seasons are moderated by the lake. The Okanagan's char-

Irrigation makes the Okanagan Valley one of B.C.'s prime agricultural areas. D. Clemson Armstrong, Photo 33821, Vancouver Public Library

acteristic late spring keeps fruit blossoms from opening before temperatures are warm enough. Its low relative humidity makes some diseases, such as apple scab, less likely than elsewhere in B.C. Warm days and cool nights "colour-up" Okanagan apples. The only missing ingredient is rainfall at critical times in the crop cycles. This lack of groundwater is compensated for by irrigation from the lake.

So Okanagan Lake is critical to fruit-growers. Because of it, temperatures in the valley seldom drop below -23°C, the point at which the tender flower buds of peach, cherry and apricot start to die. Actually, the trees can stand such cold in, say, mid-December. Later on, in spring, the more-developed blossoms can't stand it.

Any sudden change in the weather – hot or cold, dry or wet – is likely to hurt orchards. The last day of January 1988 was unseasonably warm, 16°C. Overnight, temperatures plunged to -18°C. All the apricot blossoms were killed. Two years later, the heavy rains of June 1990 caused many south Okanagan cherry varieties to be abandoned on the trees from splitting: the fruit simply absorbed too much water.

Hail is, of course, an orchardist's nightmare. The Okanagan Valley's worst hailstorm devastated an all-time bumper crop of apples, pears, peaches, apricots and prunes in 15 minutes during the late afternoon of July 29, 1946. The hailstones measured as much as 5 cm in diameter and weighed 85 g. Not only did they

Orchardists used to fend off frost with smudgepots. Now wind machines keep air moving to protect trees. Environment Canada

reduce tree-borne fruit to shreds, they shattered greenhouses and drove people from the streets as far away as Revelstoke.

If fruit-growers' livelihoods depend on the weather, so do sailors' lives: winter- and spring-season fishermen take their lives into their hands every time they venture out. Especially around the Queen Charlottes, where for much of the year the weather is determined by the Aleutian Low, which can generate vicious storms with winds of more than 100 km/h. During the early 1970s, prices in

Frost Chart

	Latest Last Spring Frost	Average Last Spring Frost	Earliest First Fall Frost	Average First Fall Frost	Average Frost-Free Days
Abbotsford	May 28	April 28	Sept 13	Oct 19	174
Castlegar	May 25	May 1	Sept 13	Oct 5	156
Cranbrook	July 12	May 26	July 18	Sept 14	110
Fort St. John	June 26	May 20	Aug 15	Sept 13	115
Hope	May 14	April 16	Sept 27	Nov 2	199
Kamloops	May 29	April 25	Sept 12	Oct 9	166
Kelowna	July 1	April 30	Aug 10	Oct 8	160
Kimberley	July 7	June 4	July 22	Sept 6	94
Nanaimo	May 30	April 21	Sept 25	Oct 25	186
Penticton	June 13	May 8	Sept 12	Oct 4	148
Prince George	July 7	June 6	July 31	Aug 31	85
Prince Rupert	May 25	May 11	Sept 24	Oct 15	156
Revelstoke	July 8	May 11	Aug 11	Oct 8	149
Smithers	July 10	June 6	July 22	Sept 6	91
Tofino	May 6	April 14	Sept 27	Nov 4	203
Vancouver	April 30	March 31	Oct 2	Nov 13	216
Vernon	June 13	April 29	Sept 6	Oct 4	157
Williams Lake	July 2	June 6	Aug 19	Sept 9	94

Weather station temperatures are taken several feet above the ground. Gardeners should use extremes rather than averages since ground temperature is cooler.

Japan for herring roe soared and a single boatload of these pungent little fish could make the crew as much money as a normal season's fishing. Five fishermen were killed during an Easter weekend storm in the Strait of Georgia in March 1975, and 10 more lost their lives north of Prince Rupert in December 1979. Of all the British Columbians whose lives are ruled by our erratic and whimsical weather, the stake fishermen have is the most profound.

A Fisherman in his Element

John reached up to a small, round, wooden-based barometer that was hanging between two pilothouse windows and casually moved the top needle on its old-fashioned china face from the Gothic print of STORMY to RAIN, and said, "Years ago, I was in Winter Harbour on the west coast of Vancouver Island, tied up to a great big beautiful troller who was making really big money at that time. I just couldn't understand having to support such a huge boat. As long as I could pay all my expenses and educate my kids and save a little money, I just wanted to go on fishing, because I loved it. Another friend told me he wanted to extract a certain number of dollars from the ocean by a certain age and then quit, but I have never had any idea of ending fishing so long as I was healthy. It's a way of life for me. I just want to take things easier as I go along. The people and the sea life of the coast and all its rain and fog and beautiful sunrises and sunsets become part of you and you part of it. It's indivisible. That was quite a squall we went through. On the water you have to keep in mind all the time that *the sea is out to get you*. Treat the sea as if it is *always* trying to get you. It's the only way to survive. You can never really relax. Never!"

He got up and poured himself another drink and turned around to face me, holding his mug in midair. "Say, do you get seasick?" he asked.

– *Fishing With John,* © Edith Iglauer, 1988
Harbour Publishing, 1988

Experience is the great teacher. Smell the MacMillan-Bloedel Harmac pulp mill south of Nanaimo enough times, have it rain soon afterward enough times, and you begin to associate the two. Have your grandmother tell you that the moon on its back holds water, and you begin to look for rain during the last phase of the moon. (Live where it rains a lot and you are unlikely to see the moon often enough to connect it with wet weather. In that case, who cares?)

Animals and Weather

Kelowna: "If you have ever lived near coyotes and listened to them attentively, you will know that whenever they start yipping and howling en masse, the weather is going to change – usually within 24-48 hours and more often from good weather to bad."

Same with dogs. Eric Sloane was a bestselling author in the 1940s and '50s of books about the weather including *Look at the Sky and Tell the Weather*. His dog's behaviour, like many animals', often signalled stormy weather. Dogs, like coyotes, are more capable of scenting trails before storms, Sloane figured, because when air pressure drops, odors that have been pressed to the ground or held within their sources are freed up.

Penticton: "If the cows are lying down in a herd, then there's going to be a change in the weather."

Similkameen Valley: "The ranchers all along the Similkameen River from Keremeos to Hedley read the mountain goats like fishermen read their barometers. You see them making their way down into the sagebrush and a storm's coming. They start moving back up and it's going to get hot."

– Terry Glavin
The Vancouver Sun

Kelowna: "When horses are standing together, all facing in the same direction, tails to the wind, a storm is on the way – even though the sun's still shining."

Pender Harbour: John Daly, salmon troller, on cats as weather forecasters, "If you start a cat on a boat when it's a kitten, it can be quite useful. I had a Norwegian pal who used his cat as a barometer. Joe was a real tough fisherman, with this very small boat, who trolled a long way offshore. He told me, 'I used to watch my cat, and whenever the cat spat at me and ran up the mast and clawed hell out of it, I knew it was really going to blow and I'd better head for shelter. Then somebody gave me a barometer, and every time it dropped a long way down I started running in. Often the wind didn't come, and I lost money. So I got fed up and threw the barometer overboard and said 'Yaw, I go back to the cat.'"

Fishing With John, © Edith Iglauer, 1988
Harbour Publishing, 1988

Salmo: "It's the call of the robin. When rain's coming on, they get a little shriller in their cries. A little more strident.

"I can remember one time in Salmo, about, oh, three years ago. And it was about 30-35°C, a real hot, clear day. And I'm playing baseball, I'm in centre field, and I look over at the left fielder, and I say, 'It's gonna rain.' And he looks at me like I'm nuts.

"And I say, 'Listen to the robins.'

"Sure enough, twenty minutes later, the skies cloud over, and it pours, it washes out our tournament."

Raining Cats and Dogs

The strangest rain ever to fall in B.C. consisted of tiny, winged beetles, which fell intermittently for three hours on October 14, 1934, at Rock Candy Creek (north of Grand Forks; named after a fluorspar mine whose ore has the crystalline appearance of rock candy).

Black rain fell over eastern Canada October 16, 1785, from yellow clouds accompanied by intense darkness, thought to have been caused by forest fires in west and central Ontario. Live lizards fell in Montreal during December of 1857. In May 1895, Winnipeg was showered with huge black ants the size of wasps.

– information from *The Canadian Weather Trivia Calendar*, 1987-90

Seagull, Seagull, sit on the sand;
It's a sign of rain when you're at hand.

You can tell when there's humidity in the air. Watch insects. See how low they're flying – insects that would be flying at 10 to 12 metres – and they're all of a sudden low to the ground. It shows they're picking up a lot of humidity on their wings.

Creatures of all kinds have heightened sensitivities and routinely pick up changes in air pressure or humidity that humans need instruments to measure. When they notice the change they act on it. Sometimes they become agitated. People who work outdoors learn to read those natural signs.

Using the Senses

Vancouver: When the North Shore looks much closer than usual, you can almost see the houses, that means the wind is stirred up, sea salt is suspended high in the air rather than lower at sea level, and haze is blown away.

"When you are driving over the Lion's Gate Bridge and you can see Vancouver Island, that means it's going to rain."

Visibility at sea is often best before a shower because the salt haze is dispersed much higher in unstable air, Eric Sloane explains. Distant shores appear closer:

When the hills loom green and clear, that's the time a shower's near.

New Westminster: "If you can't see Mount Baker, it's raining. If you *can* see it, it's a sign of rain." (Note: reliable only from late October to April.)

"When the smoke from the mills is going upriver, housewives do their washing and hang out their clothes. If the smoke is going downriver, they say we can't hang our clothes out today."

Powell River: "When we see the tugs tie up with the booms or with the chip barges or the sawdust barges, we know there's a storm coming, and when they take off, we know the storm is on its way (out)."

Courtenay: "My grandmother in England used to say that when there was a new moon and the moon is on its back and you can pour a cup of tea into the new moon, then it would be wet month."

The moon with a circle brings water in her beak.

Prince George: "My grandmother told me this one and she lived in Germany, but it's supposed to work all around the world. She always said that if it was a clear night and you could see the moon, if it had a halo, the next day the weather would change and you would have rain or whatever . . ."

The bigger the ring, the nearer the wet.

Actually, the ring around the moon is the product of increasing moisture in the upper atmosphere, which is itself a harbinger of a weather system moving in. In that sense, the ring *is* the bad weather it forecasts.

Nanaimo: "When you can smell the pulp mill, it's going to rain." Wind from the southeast generally brings weather systems with it. In general, if winds turn from east to southeast or southerly, look for bad weather. If from the north or west, look for good weather.

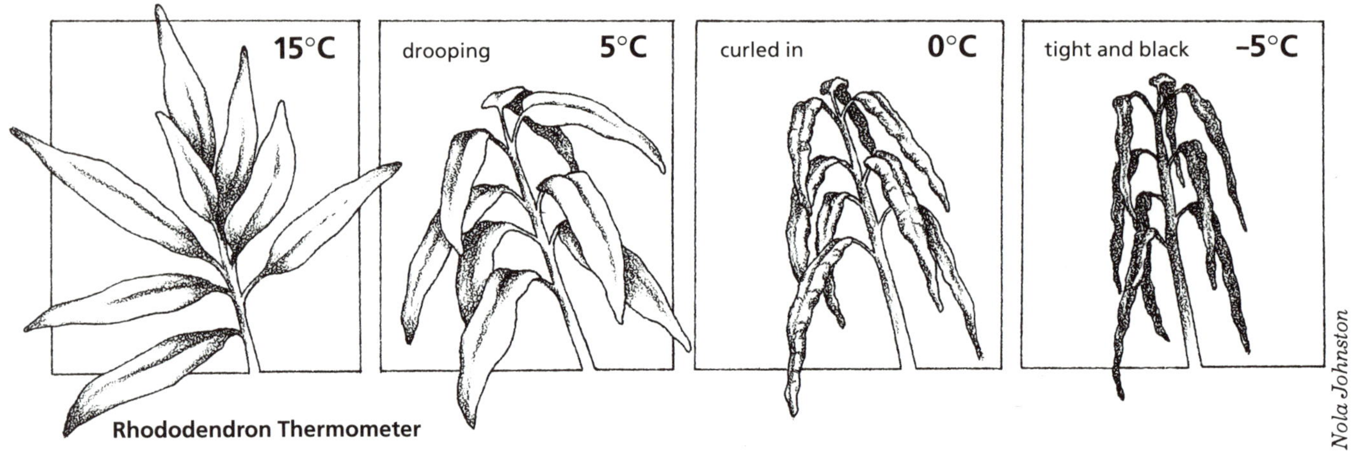

Rhododendron Thermometer

Vancouver: "I'm one of those people who can smell snow. Everybody around here laughs at me, but I can smell the snow before it will happen."

– Lucie McNeill, CBC Radio, Vancouver

How Accurate are Almanacs?

Summer is expected to be cool, with near normal precipitation or slightly below inland, and below normal in coastal areas. Brief warm spells toward the end of July, in early August and several times in September will not compensate for the cold spells in early July, mid-August, and before and after mid-September. Showers will be distributed fairly frequently."

– forecast for summer 1990, *The Old Farmer's Almanac*

In 1990 in early spring the southern Interior of B.C. was, in fact, drier than usual for the seventh straight year. Then came the rains of May and June. In the Okanagan and the Kamloops area the weather then turned perfect, causing a late snowmelt and flooding.

On the Lower Mainland a wet spring ended only on July 8th, when the fourth-longest dry spell ever recorded began. It lasted 41 days. Sunday, Aug. 12 was the hottest day of the year in Vancouver at 31.9°C – breaking the previous record by more than three degrees. And the heat wave had five more days to go.

In June it looked as if *The Old Farmer's Almanac* had guessed low about B.C.'s rainfall but might otherwise be right. By August, though, it was obvious that anyone who had gone elsewhere seeking summer sunshine on the advice of the almanac had wasted money.

When ditch and pond offend the nose,
Look for rain and stormy blows.

Invermere: "The easiest thing to predict was a chinook (an Indian word meaning snow-eater) from the shrieking that the wind made. And yes, we did get chinooks in the Windermere Valley, sometimes only minutes after the shrieking warning of the wind.

One day I decided to go skiing about a mile and a half away. I was skiing up the road when I heard this shrieking wind. I quickened my pace so I would get in a bit of skiing before the chinook spoiled the slopes, but the snow was getting pretty tacky by the time I got there. I was able to go down once, and I walked back up to the top with about six inches of snow stuck to the bottom of my skis.

I tried to go down again but it was no use, so I headed home. You could almost see the snow melt around you. By the time I got to the hill by Old Man Heath's place, dirt and grass were poking up through the snow. There had been a foot of snow along the road and five or six inches of hard pack in the ruts when I had come an hour before. The driveway at home was getting bare when I came through the gate. I had to take off my skis and carry them up to the house."

Gibsons: John Knotts of the Pacific Region Meteorological Department was staying with Muriel Haynes and her family in the 1950s. As a physiotherapist, Muriel had concluded that if more than three patients a day called in with mysterious joint pains then the weather would change. They compared predictions, and during the week that John Knotts was a visitor, her findings were more accurate than his.

Muriel says the lining of the joints is very sensitive to pressure and reacts to weather changes.

Fraser Lake: Local weatherman learns how to foretell a bad winter, "I had occasion to take the local Indian chief into a school board meeting once, and it was in the fall, and I thought, 'Well, this is a good way to see what the winter was going to be like.' He was sure to have some good old Indian lore.

"So I asked him, 'Pete, what sort of winter are we going to be having?'

"He said, 'Oh, cold one.'

"I said 'How do you know?'

"He said, 'The white man has a big wood pile.'"

Indian Weather Legends

It is not surprising that North Coast Indian mythology linked water with goodness.

From the Queen Charlottes to Puget Sound, native Indians enjoyed a relatively easy life that enabled them to build the most advanced aboriginal cultures north of Mexico. The climate was comfortable. The lush coastal rain forests gave them food, clothing and materials for solid, permanent buildings and watertight canoes. The annual salmon run provided them with an easily harvested, year-long supply of tasty protein. Water, they realized, was the basis of the Good Life, and there was no such thing as too much of it.

Even flooding meant renewal. Not only did the spring floods of the Fraser and Columbia rivers foretell the bountiful salmon spawning season, but some Indian people, such as the Squamish, believe they descended from the survivors of just such a flood. So, although it seems hard to believe, all of the bands in our region performed rituals calling for rain. Rain dances were well-known features of the plains cultures where relief from drought was critical to survival. But why didn't the original inhabitants of the wettest region in the hemisphere settle for celebrating rain? Why did they want *more* rain?

Two reasons: our summer and our winter.

Winter because winters were more severe then. Before the turn of the century the Fraser River, where it becomes shallow west of Hope, often froze over. Mid-winter rain rituals called for the warm west winds to melt the snow and ice and bring on the spring floods. Only after those floods receded would the salmon run begin. For people living on the smoked products of last year's fishing season, breakup meant the return of fresh food.

Our summers can feature periods of clear, rain-free weather that often last for months on end. Vegetation dries up. Forest fires break out. Despite our reputation for having a moist climate, most other parts of North America get more rain during the summer months.

Therefore, the most important character of Kwagiutl mythology was Thunderbird because he embodied both the supply of water and protection from evil.

Not only did Thunderbird provide the moist climate that produced some of the tallest trees in creation and the fastest-flowing rivers with a bounty of salmon, Thunderbird also did constant battle with the forces of evil. Evil was embodied in Killer Whale, lord of the seas and underworld.

Like all myths, those of the highly-intelligent peoples who lived on this coast are based on timeless truths. The legends are derived from 5000 years of observation and add up to an accurate depiction of the power of weather along the northwest Pacific Coast. People looked up and saw good and bad winds fighting it out in the heavens.

Those forces were particularly overpowering to communities that, like the Kwagiutl, lived along the outer coasts, at the mercy of Pacific storms. The legends were similar for most coastal peoples, who, of course, recognized no international boundaries and whose bands were loosely related.

Practically every native group of the northwest coast has such a flood myth, and these flood myths have much in common.

We continue to live in an ice age, during which the polar ice caps have advanced and

retreated quite frequently. During the last period of maximum advance, only about 18,000 years ago, Vancouver was covered to a depth of a kilometre of ice (Calgary and Toronto, by the way, were 3 km under). We are near the end of a 10,000-year withdrawal and it has been predicted that there will be a one-metre rise in sea level over the next century.

The last time the earth reached this stage in the retreat-advance ice age cycle, coastal lowlands, river deltas and valleys were being flooded, and myths like that of Noah's Ark became universal.

The Squamish people of Howe Sound, like recent white inhabitants of the Fraser Valley, could see the flood coming. At a council, they decided to build a giant canoe and tie it to a huge rock. The men built the canoe, working night and day, while the women made the rope by gathering cedar fibre, shredding it, rolling and chewing the strands, and working it into the strongest rope any of them had ever seen.

Every baby and small child was put into the canoe, along with a the sixteen-year-old mother of a two-week-old baby, who sat in the bow, and the bravest of their young men, who took the stern seat. No one else tried to climb into the boat, and no one wept as it floated on its tether and the waters rose over every peak in sight.

"For days the children and their young guardians saw only a world of water and sky. But the rope held. One morning they saw, far to the south, a speck on top of the water."

Through that day and night, the speck became a mountain – the one we see to our south on fine days, Mount Baker. The young man cut the rope and paddled south. By the time they arrived, its top half was dry. When the waters had fully receded, they built their lodges between the Fraser River and Georgia Strait, within sight of the mountain that had saved them.

By the way, the name Squamish means "drifted away."

– retold in Ella E. Clark, *Indian Legends of the Pacific Northwest*

Killer Whale was the lord of the seas and the underworld to BC's coastal natives. Thunderbird embodied the supply of water and did battle with Killer Whale. Nola Johnston

WEATHER AND SPORTS

Victoria and the Lower Mainland have always been hotbeds of outdoor games played in anything but earthquakes – soccer, rugby, and lacrosse. Victoria bills itself as nothing less than the amateur sports capital of Canada. In the Interior, where honest-to-goodness Canadian winters exist, skiing and amateur hockey have been important sports since before the First World War. British Columbians would rather play than watch, one reason professional sports haven't done especially well here.

Soccer and Rugby

"There's no question in my mind that the best soccer players in Canada come from B.C. because here you can train outdoors the year-round," says Bobby Lenarduzzi, coach of the Vancouver 86ers, three-time Canadian Soccer League and 1990 North American champions. "All that extra training adds up over the years."

In 1990 B.C. won the Canadian rugby championship for the eighth straight year by beating Ontario 48-9 in Ottawa. B.C.'s opponent each of those years was Ontario, a province with more than three times our population. We have won those eight final games by a total score of 269-70.

Lacrosse

When lacrosse was truly our national sport, its senior championship was a B.C. monopoly. Of all team games, lacrosse is the one that is native to B.C. The Coast Salish bands who lived in the Fraser Valley often played lacrosse on fields several miles long, with hundreds of young men on each team.

By 1905 lacrosse was fully professional in B.C. and easily the most popular sport. The New Westminster Salmonbellies, organized in 1889, held the B.C. title almost every year until 1910 and won the Canadian professional championship six times from 1908 to 1914. Canada's senior amateur championship was won by Lower Mainland or Victoria teams every year from 1911 to 1925. But by then the heyday of outdoor field lacrosse as a major spectator sport in B.C. was over.

Native Canadians made a return to their own game during the 1930s, a golden age of local lacrosse during which the North Shore Indians, who played a wide-open offensive style that was fun to watch, often packed the Denman Street Arena with more than 11,000 fans. More recently, lacrosse boomed on Vancouver Island during the 1950s, touching off a revival of the province's supremacy nationwide: Teams from southwestern B.C. have won the senior amateur championship 22 times in the last 35 years.

Track and Field

B.C. produces far more than its share of the country's track and field athletes: both of Canada's native-born world champion sprinters, Percy Williams and Harry Jerome, were from Vancouver. So is Debbie Brill, the long-time world-ranked high-jumper. Not because of our climate, though.

"It's interesting, you know, that our weather works against my particular sport," Brill says. "The fact that we have a short winter is good. You can run, but you can't practise high-jumping in the rain.

The North Shore Indians, who reclaimed their game in the 1930s. Photo CVA 99-354 City of Vancouver Archives

"Because we think it's such a wonderful climate – and it is – it's worked against us. Our winters are considered so mild that the people in charge have felt there was no need for an indoor training facility. The one place we had until recently has been turned into a weight-training gym. You can spend a whole winter here doing nothing."

Many B.C. track stars accept athletic scholarships to attend American universities, but Brill preferred to stay in B.C. In order to reach her peak fitness for important events, though, she often travelled to California for perhaps a month before a big meet. "It was just ridiculous," she says, laughing at the irony of a mild climate making it difficult to train. "There was nowhere to jump in B.C. during the winter."

Golf

The game that is the most sensitive to weather is the one that Canadians think of first when they imagine the pleasures of Lotusland.

"The golf courses (around Vancouver and Victoria) are crowded on Christmas Day," former *Vancouver Sun* editor Bruce Hutchison wrote in 1950 as a bit of one-upmanship on the rest of the country. The old joke about golf in southwestern B.C. was that former prairie dogs would shoot a round on New Year's Day and phone home to Winterpeg, gloating to their snowbound in-laws.

"When the citizens of Winnipeg are shivering in a blizzard at the corner of Portage and Main, the old men of Vancouver, not far from Georgia and Granville, will be playing giant checkers in the forest park, on a checkerboard twelve feet square," Hutchison added.

Today, nothing has changed except the number of golf courses. Thirty years ago the best Canadian professional golfer was Vancouver's Stan Leonard. At present, all three top Canadian touring pros – Dave Barr, Dick Zokol, and Ray Stewart – are from B.C.

Hang gliding near Invermere – BC's rugged topography generates supportive updrafts. Province of British Columbia

Softball

Sometimes the answer to uncertain weather, as with so many other problems in life, is simply to ignore it. Prince Rupert averages more overcast days and more days with precipitation per year than any city in Canada. If the usual rain-out rule applied, precious little softball would ever get played there.

"We just ignore the rain," says Harry Fairbrother, a Prince Rupert slo-pitch softball organizer, "and whether we're up to our ankles in water or up to our knees in mud, we play. I've seen teams that come out in their regular uniforms but mostly they dress for rain. There are some pretty awkward-looking outfits – old pants, hats, gloves (on throwing hands), raincoats. I think the worst part is trying to hold the bat in a real downpour . . ."

Swimming

For a number of years, many of the best swimmers in Canada came, appropriately enough, from the wettest inhabited place in the country, Ocean Falls, B.C. The town is virtually surrounded by water and is inundated with more than 500 cm of rain during some years, so the illustrious Ocean Falls Swim Club was a clear case of the old adage that when life gives you lemons, make lemonade.

The site, located halfway up an ocean inlet at about the same latitude as South Moresby Island in the Queen Charlottes, was ideal for a pulp and paper mill in 1909. Life in mill towns often revolves around the consumption of alcohol. The company that built Ocean Falls, a predecessor of Crown Zellerbach, decided to put the profits from the sale of beer and liquor into recreational facilities. In 1928 one of the finest heated indoor pools in Canada was built there.

A pool was the town's first priority because it was felt that drownings in the surrounding waters could be prevented if children were taught to swim. The swim club became the only game in a town where "there were no cars, no slums, no unwanted residents, and no unemployment," recalls Dr. Jack Kelso, a professor of Physical Education at the University of B.C. and one of the swim club's stars during the 1950s. Once the club realized the training advantages of its remoteness and hired its great coach, George Gate, in 1950, its athletes began to amass the most impressive record in Canadian amateur sports. Two standouts were Ralph Hutton and Sandy Gilchrist, who won 13 medals between them at the 1966 British Empire Games.

"During the years 1948 to 1974," writes Kelso in his book about the club, "of 22 national swimming teams competing in international competition, swimmers from the Ocean Falls Amateur Swim Club were members of 21. They have amassed a total of 59 medals . . . (a record) unequalled by any other swimming club in Canada during the same period."

Just as Ocean Falls' remote, watery location and climate made it, in Kelso's words,

In a place as wet as rainy Ocean Falls, there's not much to do but swim. So they built an indoor pool and produced some of Canada's best swimmers. Glenn Baglo, The Vancouver Sun

"Canada's Reservoir of Swimming Excellence," those same qualities made it a ghost town when the mill's machinery wore out. The mill closed in 1980. Among B.C.'s many ghost towns, Ocean Falls is one of the few where the sounds you hear are not creaking hinges, but splashes.

Skiing

Of all the winter sports we might logically expect British Columbians to excel in, the first that comes to mind is skiing. B.C. is a vast unmade bed of mountain ranges, set row upon row across the province. Whistler/Blackcomb has the longest continuous ski runs in North America. Helicopter skiing at high levels in the Selkirks and Monashees in southeastern B.C. attracts powder hounds from around the world.

Great slopes and great powder, like at Silver Star, makes for great fun, but not as many champions as you might think. Province of British Columbia

"You know that the Inuit have more than one hundred words for snow," Nancy Greene Raine says. "Well, skiers have almost as many. Powder, corn, fluff, silk, hard pack, cement (and Sierra cement, which is heavy wet powder), crud, crust – you get the idea – blue ice...

"You can find most of those types of snow in B.C. and many of them on the same mountain. At Whistler, it can be raining in the valley and it'll be snowing further up. In the Interior the snow is more consistent from top to bottom."

For skiers, the province is an embarrassment of riches. The season at Whistler is as long as anywhere. Not because it stays cold as long as elsewhere, but because there is so much snow it takes a long time to melt. All ski resorts near the Lower Mainland are on the windward side of their mountains – the side that gets the most snowfall. Even those resorts on the lee sides of mountains, such as Panorama (near Invermere) get enough snow. In B.C., the length of the ski season is not limited by snowfall. Usually interest in skiing falls off before the base melts.

Which is exactly the problem when it comes to developing elite racers. Recreational skiing here is so plentiful and enjoyable, why bother competing? In the single sport in which you would expect B.C. to dominate the country, this province has produced some great champions, but not many more than Ontario and Quebec.

Nancy explains:

"In many respects, kids from B.C. are at a disadvantage. In Ontario and Quebec, the mountains may not be that big, but they have world-class pitches. By setting up race courses, they can develop slalom racers as good as those anywhere else. Here, with the province so big, so many mountains, so lightly populated, junior skiers have to travel long distances in order to compete.

"There's so much challenge in the mountains, they're having so much fun in the powder, you can't drag them out of it. It seems like punishment to ask them to practise on a slalom course."

Another disadvantage for the half of B.C.'s junior skiers who live in and around Vancouver is the fact that the entire Lower Mainland skis at Whistler, which makes it difficult to set aside training runs. So, despite their isolation, junior skiers from the Interior have fared better in international competition.

Raine, the 1967-68 world champion who won gold and silver medals in the 1968 Olympics at Grenoble, grew up in Rossland. Gerry Sorensen, the women's World Cup downhill champion in 1982, came from Kimberley. Likewise, Rob Boyd of Whistler grew up in Vernon. (The late Dave Murray, one of the original Crazy Canuck downhillers, was an exception: he learned to race at Whistler.) B.C. continues to produce its share of World Cup racers, including the currently top-ranked woman, Kendra Kobelka of Revelstoke, and Felix Belcyk of Castlegar.

Al Raine, who was the women's national team coach during Nancy Greene's competitive career, developed into something of an alpine meteorologist because, he says, "you wax skis accordingly. To learn about that, you have to know the microclimates." At coaches' meetings before World Cup events, the first item on the agenda was always the weather forecast.

It helps to know, for example, that at Whistler it can be colder in the valley than on the mountain tops. It happens once or twice each season. After a prolonged cold snap with clear weather, an inversion will trap the cold air in the valley while warm or stormy weather systems pass overhead. It takes 24 to 36 hours for a major storm to push such an inversion out of the valley. The same thing happens in the East Kootenays.

Depending on humidity, Coach Raine says, the optimum temperature for ski racing is -1 or -2°C. "More water content makes it faster. As the air gets colder, snow gets colder. There are about four major wax types we use, but the colder it gets, the less effective wax is. Below -15° most people would be better to ski on the plastic base of their skis."

"Actually," Nancy replies, "at -15° you'd be better off not to be skiing at all; stay inside in front of the fire."

Baseball

Can you throw a better curveball in Vancouver than in other Pacific Coast League cities? "Very definitely," says Moe Drabowski, pitching coach for the Vancouver Canadians. In other PCL cities, such as Phoenix, Albuquerque, Las Vegas and Colorado Springs, Drabowski explains, "A breaking ball doesn't have the bite that it does here in our more humid climate."

"The atmosphere here is denser," says Grady Hall, Drabowski's prize pupil in 1990. Hall won 13 games for the Canadians despite not having much of a fastball: he did it with curves, sliders, forkballs and sinkers – pitches known in baseball as "junk." Vancouver is a junkballer's paradise.

Nat Bailey Stadium is a great place to throw junk balls, but a tough place to hit. It's all because of Vancouver's wet, heavy air. Dan Scott, The Vancouver Sun

When the hitters do get good wood on the ball, it doesn't carry as far in the denser air. High-altitude PCL cities, such as Colorado Springs and Albuquerque are hitters' havens because of their thinner air, in which a batted ball carries farther. Phoenix, in the Arizona desert, is dry. On the other hand dry or thin air makes life difficult for pitchers who depend on breaking pitches, as Hall does.

Like any lifetime resident of Vancouver, Chicago native Grady Hall is always happy to come home to our greener fields. "There's a lot of weather here," he adds, smiling.

Hockey

In 1912 ice hockey came to the two least likely places in Canada – Victoria and Vancouver. On January 5 of that year the Denman Street Arena, one of the first two artificial ice rinks in Canada (built simultaneously with one in Victoria), was opened with an 8-3 win by the hometown Millionaires over the New Westminster Royals. It was billed as the largest indoor sports facility in the world.

The Denman Street Arena (right) in Vancouver brought Canadian hockey indoors and changed the game forever. Photo CVA 342-918, City of Vancouver Archives

In retrospect, hockey in Victoria and Vancouver never regained the giddy heights it achieved in the game's first few years. The Vancouver Millionaires, with that era's Gretzky, Cyclone Taylor, won the Stanley Cup in 1915 and reached the finals in five of the eight seasons thereafter. Their National Hockey League successors, the Canucks, have had two winning seasons in their first 20.

Although it hasn't helped the Canucks much, it is true that B.C. has become an important producer of major-league hockey talent. Until the 1980s, most NHL players hailed from the prairies, northern Ontario, or Quebec. Coastal B.C.'s gentle climate was not conducive to producing elite hockey players. Even after three NHL expansions in six years, there were only about two dozen B.C. natives playing major-league hockey in 1973-74. The best-known were goalie Cesare Maniago of Trail and the Watson brothers from Smithers, Jim and Joe, defencemen with Philadelphia.

But by 1990 there were more than 100 B.C. players listed in the *NHL Guide and Record Book*. Enough of them are stars to make possible, for the first time, a B.C.-born NHL All-Star team led by Detroit's Steve Yzerman (from Cranbrook), Edmonton's Glenn Anderson (Burnaby) and Boston's Cam Neely (Comox) and Andy Moog (Penticton). The difference is the presence of new artificial ice rinks in most neighborhoods in the bigger cities, and community centres in towns from Duncan to Campbell River along the east coast of Vancouver Island.

Football

Canadian football is another sport that was once alien to most of the province. It has been played like a foreign game for most of the time since 1954, when the B.C. Lions were formed. Empire Stadium, their first home, was a quagmire when it opened and throughout its life had the wind characteristics of a pinball machine as the prevailing westerlies struck the west stands and eddies spun over the field through the open north and south ends to meet at the 55-yard line. Having the wind come straight out of the north was more predictable, but not necessarily preferable. Only twice in 29 years did the Lions make the Grey Cup final during the Empire Stadium years, bringing it home in 1964.

"I would rather play in six inches of manure than the wind we used to get in Vancouver,"

If You Build It, They Will Come

Ice Hockey? On Canada's Riviera? Yes. With the value of real estate along Granville Street doubling annually before the First World War, anything seemed possible – even making ice in a semi-tropical climate. In 1912 hockey was the latest sensation on the west coast.

In cities where ice came by sail from faraway glaciers and was usually used for keeping meat fresh, the introduction of the world's fastest game required new technology: the first artificial ice rinks in Canada. They were built at the same time in Victoria and Vancouver by hockey's great innovators, the Patrick brothers.

Lester and Frank Patrick learned hockey in Montreal's toney Westmount district. Both were stars: Lester played in the 1906 Stanley Cup winning Montreal Wanderers; Frank was a defenceman on the McGill team that beat Harvard in the first international intercollegiate hockey game that year.

Their father, Joe Patrick, had sold his Quebec sawmill in 1903, relocated to Nelson, and made a second fortune by selling that mill in 1911. For being his lead hands at the Nelson mill, Joe gave $25,000 each to Lester and Frank, and steered Frank into a lumber brokerage deal that made him another $35,000. (These figures can be multiplied by 20 to approximate their current value.)

The brothers missed hockey. The idea of starting a new league, to play in their own buildings, in virgin hockey territory, appealed to Joe and Frank. Lester, who thought the financial risk too great but was outvoted, went along. Lester took Victoria, Frank took Vancouver, and a third franchise was bankrolled in New Westminster. Lester was 27 at the time; Frank 25.

"They were laying it all on the line in what surely would be the most daring, ambitious and imaginative scheme of its kind in the history of sport," wrote Eric Whitehead in *Hockey's Royal Family*, his biography of the Patricks. It was called the Pacific Coast Hockey Association.

Vancouver's Denman Street Arena, which sat 10,500, was "The globe's largest indoor sports emporium" when it opened in 1912. Whitehead calculates that it was capable of "comfortably accommodating more than 10 percent of the urban population it was built to serve." It cost $110,000 to build. As a sideline, the Patricks sold blocks of ice made in the arena basement.

The best National Hockey Association players were lured west by the offer of doubled salaries. Among them was Fred (Cyclone) Taylor, known as "the Ty Cobb of Hockey." With Taylor and the rest of a lineup of which *every player* is in the Hockey Hall of Fame, the Vancouver Millionaires won the city's only Stanley Cup in 1915.

The league's legacy to hockey is immense. It introduced the blue lines, which made forward passing possible; pioneered numbered jerseys; and allowed goalies new freedom to play outside their creases, freeze the puck, and fall to the ice to make saves. With the number of whistle stoppages reduced by these rules, the PCHA began allowing substitutions on the fly. Frank Patrick saw the winning goal in an English polo match scored on a penalty shot, and introduced the idea to hockey. The PCHA also gave the game such refreshing team names as the Portland Rosebuds and Spokane Canaries.

Having long since pioneered bringing winter indoors, Frank Patrick had an inspiration in 1948 to play outdoor spectator sports in what he called a "domed stadium," Whitehead tells us. The idea is probably as old as sports. But Frank Patrick was the one who patented it.

"It is unbelievable in this day and age," Frank Patrick wrote in the notes that accompanied the plans that accompanied his patent application, "that the scheduling of sports should be governed by the vagaries of the weather."

Nowhere in this hemisphere do weather vagaries match those of coastal B.C. But it was not for another 37 years that B.C. Place Stadium eliminated weather as a factor in local professional sports when it opened in 1983. In all the celebrations, the name of Frank Patrick went unmentioned.

But he is not entirely forgotten. Both Frank and Lester Patrick are enshrined in the Hockey Hall of Fame.

"I'd rather play knee-deep in . . . " Vancouver's Empire Stadium was not loved by the athletes who had to play football there. Vancouver weather, poor drainage, and the wind tunnel effect of the stands made it a nightmare. Ross Kenward, The Province

recalls the Lions' first coach, Annis Stukus.

"We'd try to have the gale behind us in the fourth quarter, cross our fingers, and play like hell. It was best to run the short stuff, try to stay more on the ground because then you'd have ball control. A passing team was at a real disadvantage in those Empire Stadium monsoons."

Empire's replacement, B.C. Place, was Canada's first covered stadium, an idea that appeared to make so much sense that it was first thought of in Vancouver as early as 1948. It made the Lions championship contenders as soon as it opened in 1983. They made the final that year and won the Cup for a second time in 1984.

It is significant that the best B.C.-born football player ever is not a lineman or back, but a kicking specialist. Lui Passaglia's claim to fame was that he grew up playing soccer and was able to transfer his kicking expertise to the Lions so successfully that he became, in 1990, the highest-scoring professional football player ever – in any league, at any time.

In 1983 Passaglia became immune to the weather in the home games he played at B.C. Place: he set a record for the average length of his punts, a phenomenal 50.2 yards, with one kick of *93* yards.

By the late 1980s, though, the Lions had reverted to form on the field and were deep in debt off it. Because, after all, on a nice sunny summer evening in Vancouver, who wants to sit indoors watching Toronto ride roughshod over the home team?

Conversion Charts

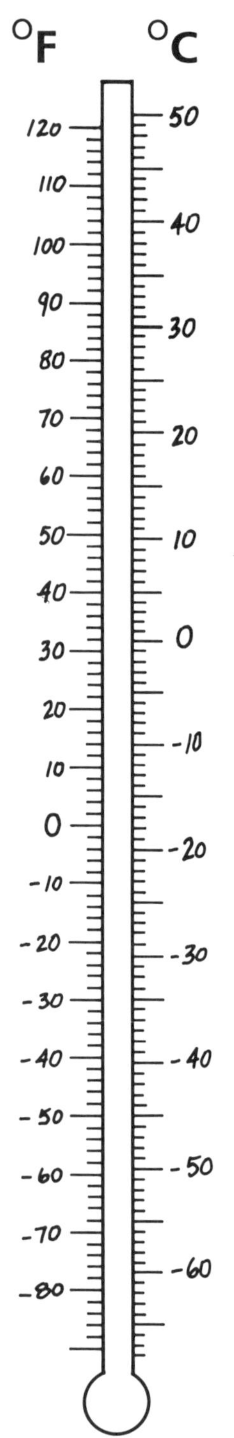

To convert Fahrenheit to Celsius, subtract 32 and multiply by 5 / 9.

To convert Celsius to Fahrenheit, multiply by 9 / 5 and add 32.

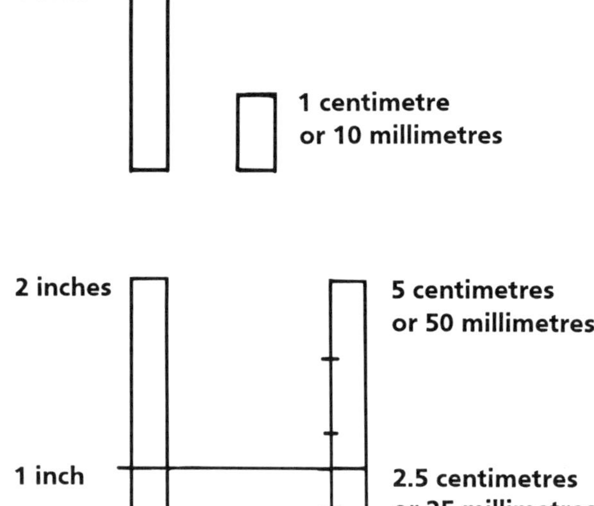

To convert inches to centimetres, multiply by 2.5.
To convert inches to millimetres, multiply by 25.
To convert centimetres to inches, multiply by .4.
To convert millimetres to inches, multiply by .04.

Conversion Charts

1/10 scale

1 foot .31 metre

1 metre 3.3 feet

To convert feet to metres, multiply by .31.
To convert metres to feet, multiply by 3.3.

1/10,000 scale

1 mile 5280 feet 1609 metres

1 kilometre 3281 feet 1000 metres

1 nautical mile 6076 feet 1852 metres

To convert miles to kilometres, multiply by 1.6.
To convert kilometres to miles, multiply by .6.

Weather Statistics Around the Province

Cranbrook

	Jan	Feb	Mar	Apr	May	June	July	Aug	Sept	Oct	Nov	Dec	Year
Total Precipitation (mm)	54	38	28	28	43	46	28	35	29	25	40	60	451
Average Number of Days with Precipitation	13	9	9	9	10	10	6	8	9	9	10	13	115
Average Daily Maximum Temperature	- 4	2	6	12	18	22	27	26	20	12	3	-2	12
Average Daily Minimum Temperature	-14	-10	-7	-1	3	7	9	8	4	-1	-7	-11	-2
Maximum Recorded Temperature	10	12	21	30	31	34	39	37	34	28	16	13	39
Minimum Recorded Temperature	- 41	-37	-30	-20	-12	-3	-1	0	- 6	-12	-32	-34	- 41
Average Hours Bright Sunshine	79	103	165	217	256	284	330	278	216	170	83	63	2243

Fort Saint John

	Jan	Feb	Mar	Apr	Mar	June	July	Aug	Sept	Oct	Nov	Dec	Year
Total Precipitation (mm)	36	27	30	22	39	68	77	60	39	28	31	36	493
Average Number of Days with Precipitation	14	11	12	8	9	12	12	10	11	9	11	13	132
Average Daily Maximum Temperature	-13	-7	-2	8	16	19	21	20	15	9	-2	-9	6
Average Daily Minimum Temperature	-22	-16	-11	-2	4	8	10	9	4	0	-10	-17	- 4
Maximum Recorded Temperature	11	13	14	28	30	32	33	33	30	26	18	14	33
Minimum Recorded Temperature	- 47	- 42	-37	-29	-11	-1	2	-1	-13	-21	-36	- 41	- 47
Average Hours Bright Sunshine	77	111	160	233	286	282	302	272	178	139	89	65	2192

Penticton

	Jan	Feb	Mar	Apr	May	June	July	Aug	Sept	Oct	Nov	Dec	Year
Total Precipitation (mm)	32	20	17	21	29	28	21	27	18	15	24	31	283
Average Number of Days with Precipitation	13	9	7	6	9	8	6	7	7	7	9	12	100
Average Daily Maximum Temperature	0	4	9	15	21	25	29	27	22	15	6	2	15
Average Daily Minimum Temperature	-5	-3	-1	2	6	10	12	12	8	3	0	-3	3
Maximum Recorded Temperature	13	16	22	29	32	37	41	39	34	29	19	14	41
Minimum Recorded Temperature	-27	-27	-18	-7	- 6	0	2	3	-3	-8	-19	-28	-28
Average Hours Bright Sunshine	48	75	140	211	246	263	311	270	211	157	60	39	2032

Weather Statistics Around the Province

Prince George

	Jan	Feb	Mar	Apr	May	June	July	Aug	Sept	Oct	Nov	Dec	Year
Total Precipitation (mm)	57	39	37	27	47	67	60	69	59	59	51	57	628
Average Number of Days with Precipitation	17	13	13	10	12	14	13	13	13	14	16	18	166
Average Daily Maximum Temperature	- 8	-1	4	10	16	20	22	21	16	10	1	- 4	9
Average Daily Minimum Temperature	-17	-11	-7	-2	3	6	8	7	4	0	-7	-12	-2
Maximum Recorded Temperature	13	13	18	30	32	34	34	33	29	25	16	12	34
Minimum Recorded Temperature	-50	-45	-38	-26	- 8	-3	-2	- 4	-12	-26	- 42	- 46	-50
Average Hours Bright Sunshine	59	87	138	203	252	260	293	253	160	110	65	47	1926

Prince Rupert

	Jan	Feb	Mar	Apr	May	June	July	Aug	Sept	Oct	Nov	Dec	Year
Total Precipitation (mm)	228	222	201	190	140	130	103	158	233	365	268	284	2523
Average Number of Days with Precipitation	20	19	21	19	18	17	16	16	18	24	22	23	233
Average Daily Maximum Temperature	3	6	7	9	12	14	16	17	15	11	7	5	10
Average Daily Minimum Temperature	- 4	-1	-1	2	4	7	10	10	7	5	0	-2	3
Maximum Recorded Temperature	13	18	17	23	27	26	28	29	24	21	19	19	29
Minimum Recorded Temperature	-24	-17	-17	-7	-2	1	3	3	-2	- 6	-18	-23	-24
Average Hours Bright Sunshine	48	63	94	135	189	151	143	138	117	65	50	32	1224

Revelstoke

	Jan	Feb	Mar	Apr	May	June	July	Aug	Sept	Oct	Nov	Dec	Year
Total Precipitation (mm)	177	95	61	51	54	78	52	59	81	84	115	154	1063
Average Number of Days with Precipitation	25	18	15	13	14	15	13	13	16	17	19	24	202
Average Daily Maximum Temperature	-3	2	6	13	20	23	27	26	19	10	3	-1	12
Average Daily Minimum Temperature	-9	-5	-3	1	5	9	11	11	7	3	-3	-7	2
Maximum Recorded Temperature	11	13	22	28	37	36	41	38	37	26	15	17	41
Minimum Recorded Temperature	-34	-32	-22	-15	-7	-2	1	- 6	-7	-12	-23	-33	-34
Average Hours Bright Sunshine	44	56	102	179	213	216	268	243	151	90	42	27	1628

Weather Statistics Around the Province

Tofino

	Jan	Feb	Mar	Apr	May	June	July	Aug	Sept	Oct	Nov	Dec	Year
Total Precipitation (mm)	404	366	372	234	143	102	86	114	163	392	432	479	3288
Average Number of Days with Precipitation	21	19	20	18	13	11	9	11	13	19	22	23	199
Average Daily Maximum Temperature	7	9	9	11	14	16	18	18	17	13	10	8	13
Average Daily Minimum Temperature	1	2	2	4	6	9	10	11	9	6	3	2	5
Maximum Recorded Temperature	14	19	18	22	26	32	33	31	29	24	21	16	33
Minimum Recorded Temperature	-15	-7	-5	-2	0	2	4	4	-1	-2	-7	-12	-15
Average Hours Bright Sunshine	66	72	139	180	216	220	224	188	170	134	64	52	1723

Vancouver

	Jan	Feb	Mar	Apr	May	June	July	Aug	Sept	Oct	Nov	Dec	Year
Total Precipitation (mm)	154	115	101	60	52	45	32	41	67	114	150	182	1113
Average Number of Days with Precipitation	20	16	16	13	10	10	6	8	10	15	18	21	163
Average Daily Maximum Temperature	5	8	9	13	17	19	22	22	18	14	9	6	14
Average Daily Minimum Temperature	0	1	2	5	8	11	13	13	10	6	3	1	6
Maximum Recorded Temperature	14	15	19	24	29	31	32	33	29	24	18	15	33
Minimum Recorded Temperature	-18	-16	-9	-3	1	4	7	6	0	-3	-12	-18	-18
Average Hours Bright Sunshine	54	82	129	181	246	239	307	256	183	121	69	48	1920

Victoria

	Jan	Feb	Mar	Apr	May	June	July	Aug	Sept	Oct	Nov	Dec	Year
Total Precipitation (mm)	154	99	72	39	29	29	18	27	40	78	131	157	873
Average Number of Days with Precipitation	19	16	16	12	10	9	5	7	9	14	18	20	155
Average Daily Maximum Temperature	6	8	10	13	17	19	22	21	19	14	9	7	14
Average Daily Minimum Temperature	0	1	2	4	7	9	11	11	9	6	3	1	5
Maximum Recorded Temperature	15	18	20	24	29	33	36	34	31	26	18	16	36
Minimum Recorded Temperature	-16	-15	-9	- 4	-1	2	4	4	-1	- 4	-13	-14	-16
Average Hours Bright Sunshine	64	86	144	180	256	258	329	274	195	144	78	52	2059

GLOSSARY

Air mass

A large mass of air having uniform characteristics of temperature and humidity.

Aleutian Low

A semi-permanent low pressure area in the northeast Pacific that influences weather in western North America.

Atmospheric pressure

The force exerted by the weight of the air. For example, a square inch column of air from sea level to the top of the atmosphere weighs 6.7 kg. But, if the air is warmed, its molecules become excited and push away from each other and the air expands. Then there are fewer molecules in the same space; it weighs less. Because this warm air weighs less it exerts less pressure.

Unfortunately one cannot simply conclude that cold air coming from the arctic is high pressure. Because the atmosphere is so deep, the pressure at high altitude doesn't always correspond to the temperature at the surface of the earth. Cold weather can be accompanied by low pressure.

Barometer

An instrument that measures atmospheric pressure.

Beaufort wind scale

A scale of 0 to 17 measuring wind velocity, originally devised by Admiral Sir Francis Beaufort of the British Navy in 1806.

Cold front

The forward edge of a cold air mass that is displacing warmer air.

Cyclone

A low pressure centre that is surrounded by higher pressure accompanied by a counterclockwise wind in northern latitudes. In the southern latitudes the accompanying wind blows clockwise.

Freezing rain

Very cold rain that freezes on impact with solid objects when air temperature is below freezing.

Front

The boundary between warm and cold air masses usually associated with a change in weather (wind shift, temperature change, clearing skies, etc.). Think of a battlefield, often called a front, where opposing forces meet.

Gale

A wind with the velocity of 34-40 knots (Force 8 on the Beaufort Scale).

Gust

A sudden and brief increase in wind velocity, shorter than a squall.

High

An area of high pressure usually associated with good weather.

Hurricane

A violent cyclone with winds of 60-83 knots. Hurricanes usually occur in the subtropics but occasionally move north.

Inversion

When temperatures increase with altitude instead of the usual decrease.

Jet stream

A strong narrow stream of wind in the atmosphere.

Knot

A unit of speed in the nautical system. A knot is equal to 1 nautical mile per hour (1852 metres or 1.2 miles on land).

Low

An area of low pressure which is usually a storm centre and whose front is preceded by unsettled weather: cloud, strong winds and precipitation.

Mean temperature

The mean temperature is the average temperature during a given period, usually a day, month or year. For example, the mean temperature for Kamloops for July is the average of all the daily highs and lows for that month over all the years it has been recorded.

Microclimate

The climate of a particular area that could be as small as your backyard.

Monsoons

Land and sea winds that change with the seasons rather than the time of day.

Orographic effect

Occurs when a moist air current is forced to rise over a mountain which cools it and causes condensation. See *Rain shadow.*

Pacific High

A semi-permanent high pressure area between Hawaii and California that in summer blocks storms from the B.C. coast. In winter it is not as effective because it moves south.

Precipitation

Any moisture that falls from the sky: rain, drizzle, sleet, snow and hail but not cloud, fog or mist.

Pressure

See *Atmospheric pressure.*

Prevailing wind

Caused by the rotation of the planet. Prevailing westerlies are the dominant west-to-east motion of the earth's atmosphere over the middle latitudes.

Rain shadow

In B.C., moisture-laden winds come from the west, dump rain on the west sides of the mountains and leave the east slopes dry or in the rain shadow. The Okanagan Valley is in the rain shadow of the Coast Mountains. See *Orographic effect.*

Relative humidity

The ratio of the amount of moisture in the air to the maximum the air could hold at a given temperature and pressure, usually expressed as a percentage.

Ridge

A tongue-like extension of a high pressure area usually associated with good weather.

Squall

A sudden and intense increase in wind velocity that lasts longer than a gust.

Tornado

A violently rotating funnel of air that moves along a narrow path. It causes devastation because of its high wind velocity – up to 200 knots – and its forceful updraft, which can heave heavy objects into the air.

Typhoon

A hurricane in the west Pacific.

Warm front

The forward edge of a relatively warm air mass that is displacing a colder one.

Westerlies

See *Prevailing wind.*

INDEX

Order Form

If you'd like more copies of *Phil Reimer's B.C. Weather Book,* fill out the form and send it to:

Phil Reimer Communications,
P.O. Box 2141,
Vancouver, B.C.
V6B 3T8

Books are $9.95 + $1.50 for postage and handling + $.70 for G.S.T ($12.15 total).

Please send me __________ copy/copies

Enclosed is a cheque or money order for
$12.15 x _______

Total _______

Name: ____

Address:____

____

City & Province: __________________________________

Postal Code: ______________________________________